THE WELLER WAY

The Weller Way

The story of the Weller Streets Housing Co-operative

ALAN McDONALD
for the Weller Streets Housing Co-operative

with a Foreword by
His Royal Highness The Prince of Wales,
KG, KT, GCB

faber and faber
LONDON · BOSTON

First published in 1986 by
Faber and Faber Limited
3 Queen Square London WC1N 3AU

Typeset by Wilmaset, Birkenhead, Wirral
Printed in Great Britain by
Whitstable Litho Ltd, Whitstable, Kent
All rights reserved

British Library Cataloguing in Publication Data

McDonald, Alan
The Weller way.
1. Housing, Co-operative—England—Liverpool
(Merseyside)
I. Title
334'.1'0942753   HD7287.72.G72L5

ISBN 0-571-13963-9

Contents

List of Illustrations

Except for the *Guardian* picture, taken by Denis Thorpe, all photographs and drawings are by Bill Halsall of the Wilkinson Hindle Halsall Lloyd Partnership.

Foreword by HRH The Prince of Wales

When I went to visit the Weller Streets Housing Co-operative in a run-down area of Liverpool in December 1984 I was electrified by the atmosphere I encountered. I hadn't come across anything quite like it before. The residents had been living in a slum clearance area and were due to be dispersed throughout the city by the Council. With the expert help of their own architect and other advisers they fought their way through the seemingly impenetrable entanglements of red tape and official opposition until they finally succeeded in building the houses *they* wanted in the kind of layout *they* liked. The result was what amounted to a very attractive village (containing part of the original slum community), nestling like an oasis in the midst of a barren, urban desert. The residents I visited, who feature so prominently in this book, all told me that their new situation was like a dream come true; in some cases after waiting for *25 years* to be rehoused. The fact that they were now responsible for the maintenance of their properties also contributed enormously to the virtual elimination of the vandalism which had previously been so rife in the area.

It is, I know, easy to become over-enthusiastic about a particular way of tackling a problem and I wouldn't go so far as to say that housing co-operatives are the only answer to the dreadful problems of inner city housing and the appalling conditions that people have had to endure in some of our major cities, but they seem to me to provide a very important part of the answer. The Weller Street residents have conclusively proved that, with professional advice and assistance (in this case from an architect in Liverpool), so-called 'ordinary people' can create the kind of surroundings that they and their neighbours would like to have. It does not require a bureaucratic organization to decide such matters for them. I also believe that there is a great deal of latent talent, skill and enterprise in the decaying parts of our cities waiting to be unleashed. The value of housing co-operatives is that they can help to provide the impetus to unleash all that potential for regeneration and ensure that people can live their lives in a more fulfilling way. It is instructive, in this regard, to recall the words of a former president of the United States, Thomas Jefferson, who was also an architect – 'I know of no safe depository of the ultimate powers of society but the people themselves, and if we think them not enlightened enough to exercise their control with a wholesome discretion, the remedy is not to take it from them, but to inform their discretion.'

What I saw of these schemes filled me with enthusiasm and I reflected a great deal on the immense possibilities they conjured up. I only hope that the experience of the members of the Weller Streets Housing Co-operative will encourage more people in similar situations, who may be at their wits' end to know how to escape from a bureaucratic cul-de-sac, and perhaps inspire them with the self-confidence to discover previously hidden talents and abilities, which could spill over into other regenerative enterprises. I hope, too, that it will prove to be an encouragement for the architectural profession to see the value of living and working with a community in order to help them design a more attractive urban setting which responds to our human and aesthetic needs.

This applies not only to new-build housing co-operatives like Weller Street, where I was greatly impressed by the actual design of the houses and the individual nature of each of them, but also to the restoration and improvement of older terraced houses, many built at the beginning of the nineteenth century, which in most parts of this country have been systematically demolished as being unfit for human habitation, thereby destroying that indefinable sense of community, as well as removing houses that had a definite attraction because they had 'character'. There have been several restoration and improvement schemes in different parts of the country in the past ten years and these have shown what can be achieved by the residents working with an architect and sympathetic builders to achieve the kind of individual improvements they want. Such schemes of urban renewal have also demonstrated what can be done when a local authority shows a practical and responsive attitude in their interpretation of the building regulations for older buildings and does not insist on rigid and inflexible standards. The end result, of course, is that the wishes of the individual residents are accommodated and they have homes to be proud of. And if people (chiefly through their own efforts and achievement) have homes they can be proud of, then they will be cared for, and vandalism, break-ins and so on will become things of the past.

It must surely be our aim in this country to try and create, and restore, a real sense of community in inner city areas, based on taking account of the individual needs of residents, and by ensuring that the physical surroundings are on a suitably intimate scale to engender that community feeling, encompassing all age groups. If anyone wants to see how it can be achieved I suggest that they read this down-to-earth account of the Weller Street experience. It might raise your spirits, as it has raised mine . . . !

Introduction

Park Road, the home of the Weller Streets Housing Co-operative, was named after Toxteth Park. Two centuries ago the rich merchants and adventurers and men of commerce of Liverpool would ride with their families up the road, through woodland, to admire the view across the Mersey estuary from the Dingle.

Now Park Road is lined with shops and pubs, with older terraced houses and Council flats and maisonettes. Now the name Toxteth isn't associated with a park. As Arthur Roberts, a lifelong resident of the area, and a member of the Weller Streets Co-op from the start, puts it: 'There's this Pyramid Game on the telly. They put a name up and you have to think of another name to match it. It said "riots" and somebody said Toxteth. And my stomach turned over. I tell you, I felt mad.'

Locally nearly everyone – whether or not they sympathized with the riots of 1981 – feels some kind of anger at someone in power. Unemployment has steadily increased over the last ten years: over two in five of the adult male population are out of work. The rents for a grotty Council walk-up flat or maisonette have soared, partly because of centrally imposed cuts in housing subsidies. Despite the efforts of planners and housing managers, great stretches of the area have an air of shabby dereliction. Trees planted by the Council have taken root here and there. New jobs haven't.

About halfway up Park Road on the left, behind the furniture depository and a row of seedy shops, is an area that, according to one ex-resident, used to be 'a great tourist spot: you could see the cathedral from the outside toilet'. Now a new housing development has replaced the old Weller Streets, where two-up two-down terraced houses stood for 120 years. For the last twenty-five years of their life the houses were blighted by clearance proposals. At the time of the Toxteth riots they were still standing, still lived in; still a cause for frustration and anger.

By contrast, half a mile up Park Road, opposite the recently modernized but still gloomy Byles Street block of walk-up flats, nestles a small modern estate quite unlike anything around it. Groups of six or seven houses in ruby-red brick are set in ten L-shaped courtyards, where bushes and shrubs are pushing up among the few parked cars. It looks like rented housing, regular and utilitarian, but it has a private, secluded feeling to it too. You don't quite feel you can wander in through the pathways, but you don't quite feel excluded either.

If you do wander in, you'll come to a road through the estate called 'Weller Way'. Maybe you do a double-take, and think: How could I say that to the cabby on a Saturday night? When he says, 'Where are you going, pal?' and you say 'Weller Way'?

This is the Weller Streets Housing Co-operative: born out of frustration and anger, a sense of difference, and a sense of humour. What follows is their story: of how a group of sixty-one families came to be the first new-build housing co-operative in Britain to be founded, developed and managed by its working-class members.

The sense of difference about the Weller Streets is enormous and astonishing. The idea that lives in their bricks and mortar and in the way they run their affairs – that a small group of working people can collectively take control of a substantial part of their lives, their housing – is hard to come to terms with. The members themselves still find it hard. Their leaders still constantly worry that their organization's not right, that people aren't pulling their weight, when to an outsider the continued success of the co-op is clear, and the commitment of time and energy which a substantial proportion of its members are prepared to make to it is remarkable.

Outsiders find the success hard to come to terms with too. They talk about its special 'chemistry', the 'characters' involved, adding, 'Of course, it's unrepeatable.'

The success of the Weller Streets is hard to come to terms with because it's such an unfamiliar idea. For it challenges a consensus about housing, and the politics of housing, which is shared by right, left and centre alike. Within this consensus three main types of housing predominate in late twentieth-century Britain:

1. The declining private rented sector, where landlords make profits out of tenants;
2. The Council sector, where the local State – in Scouse, the Corpie – builds, manages and controls housing for tenants and admits them on the basis of 'need';
3. The growing owner-occupied sector, where individuals who can afford it (and 60 per cent of households in the country can now, it seems, afford it) control their own housing and make their own profits, which they generally reinvest in their next house.

In addition, over the past two decades housing associations – non-profit-making, mostly paternalist bodies – have been financed and indirectly controlled by government to offer an 'alternative' to private and to Council housing.

Conservatives and socialists, within their divisions, unite in their support of this consensus: that these indeed are the choices which should be made available. They differ about the respective roles of the sectors. Conservatives have, more and more aggressively, championed owner-occupation as the road to individual freedom, and are determined to confine public housing to provision for 'special needs'. Socialists, on the other hand, have defended the general role of Council housing, and argued for more investment in its upkeep and replacement, by appealing to 'need' and 'waiting lists'.

Against this consensus, co-operatives represent an entirely different option: a form of collective ownership where no one makes any profit; a form of renting, with collective as landlord and the household as tenant, where power is not remote but local. In Eastern Europe and Scandinavia it's a common form of housing tenure. But in Britain the consensus between right and left is so strong that both ends of the political spectrum find the idea incomprehensible and, perhaps, threatening. To the right it's an initiative in self-help that won't be allowed to disturb the mainstream; to the left it's a remarkable, perhaps opportunist, experiment that won't be allowed to disturb the mainstream.

One curious result of this is that co-operatives get described as a 'middle way', and are then confused with all those other middles: middle-of-the-road, middle ground, parties of the centre. In Liverpool they became associated, in party politics, with the long period during which the Liberals, in minority power on the Council with Conservative support, espoused the cause of housing co-ops while ratcheting up Council rents, suspending Council house-building and doing nothing about the quality of service for Council tenants.

In 1983 in Liverpool the Labour Party came into power. Since then they've embarked, in the face of severe restrictions on spending from the Tory government, on an ambitious programme of Council house-building and rehabilitation. They are reorganizing housing management on an area basis; they are trying to revitalize the maintenance service for Council tenants.

But they are adamantly against housing co-ops. This is partly related to financing of repairs, and the protection of direct labour jobs. As the District Labour Party's 1984 Housing Policy Statement puts it: 'The funds are used on the properties which need the repairs, usually the older properties. The repair is carried out by direct labour. The better and newer properties are contributing to the older properties, the more new properties in the pool the better.' Thus co-ops are seen as backdoor privatization of repair work, and a loss to the 'pool' of money available for repairs (though co-ops have the financial advantage of having all capital loans that can't be repaid from rents met by 'housing association grant').

These arguments spill over into ideology. Housing co-ops in Liverpool have become identified with the 'middle way', as some kind of compromise between socialism – the collective aspirations of working people – and liberal capitalism – self-help, and the services of private sector architects, housing associations as development and managing agents, and other professionals.

For the socialists who form a majority of the leaders of the Weller Streets Co-op – Labour supporters and sympathizers, staunch trade unionists – this outcome is tragic. For they see housing co-ops as a radically different way. Some would see their co-op as an attempt to pick up a lost strand in the socialist tradition: a belief in mutual democratic organization, a belief that working people have the right and the ability to create and control their own institutions.

As such, housing co-operatives are as much a threat to the bureaucratic centralized left as they are to the bureaucratic centralized right. For they're partly founded on the underlying reality that for most people the Corpie is a kind of enemy, whoever says they're politically in control of it: an uncontrollable, paternalist animal that you try to manipulate or keep out of the way of; a child of good intentions that has taken on a life of its own.

Of course, there is a catch. If co-ops are separated from the local Council, they have to buy services from the 'private sector'. And here another 'middle' rears its ugly head: the involvement of professionals, the middle classes. And there's no doubt that the growth of co-ops has been fostered by middle-class people out of a mixture of idealism and self-interest. The Weller Streets, themselves fostered by one such group, were deeply distrustful of such people. Professionals had to demonstrate a genuine, personal commitment to the co-op before they were accepted. Eventually the Weller Streets broke off its agreement with the housing association that helped to initiate it, and decided to go it alone.

Ironically, a very similar distrust of private sector middle-class professionals helped to cause Liverpool Labour Party's rejection of the co-op idea. Weren't the architects just in it for the fees? Weren't the housing associations just in it for the business and the kudos?

And so, sadly, a local Labour Party which claims for the creed of its housing policy 'You can't control what you don't own' ends up endorsing owner-occupation and Council housing, and rejecting a form of new-build housing in which tenants genuinely own and control their own housing: a form pioneered by the Weller Streets.

Just as the co-op itself grew out of frustration and anger, so too did the importance of getting their story told, and told in their own way. As the present chairman describes his reactions to reporters who came down to see them: 'They'd come down and say, How's the system fucking assisted you? And the system hadn't given us anything. We had to wring everything out of them.'

So people in the co-op set up their own organization, the Weller Streets Publishing Company – wholly owned by co-op members – to finance the writing of this book. I'd worked for the housing bureaucracy and then for CDS, the co-op's one-time professional agents; now the publishing company asked me, as a freelance writer, to write the story. Introducing me to the committee in my new guise, Billy Floyd, the ex-chairman, gave an outline of my impossible brief: 'The only people not getting mileage out of the Weller Streets are the Weller Streets. A lot of other people are. So what we want is all the events, all the technical data, but the story: you know, the jokes, the hard graft, everything...'

I've tried to fulfil this tall order; tried to see all sides. One of my ex-colleagues in the bureaucracy said to me: 'In essence they thought, and I think still believe, that they beat the system in some way. I think in fact the system proved it could work for groups like them.'

I see what he means, but it's a dangerous point of view. For part of what he's saying is that the system can soak up all their anger and frustration, and let them have some of what they want, and then go back, undisturbed, to the way things more or less were before.

Against this I've ended up, frankly, on the co-op's side: disturbed by their anger, amazed by their creativity and persistence, shocked into sharing their feeling that an unholy alliance of bureaucrats and politicians of right, centre and left lines up against them, and working people like them, if they try to do something collectively for themselves.

Not that it's as one-dimensional as all that. The co-op made many friends and allies among the professionals they dealt with. I'd now count myself as one. This is, therefore, an account that does its best to be fair, but doesn't pretend to be objective. It's the story, told through memories and documents and a few glimpses of the characters involved, of a small group of people who saw an extraordinary idea through to achievement; a group whose experience is a testament to the possibility of real change, of changing the choices available and not just picking freely among the options the consensus is prepared to let us have. To ignore that experience is to ignore the human potential in every area like the Weller Streets, human potential going to waste. If it continues to be ignored, then the real political problems facing our cities are being ignored, the real issues people feel to be important about the way government deals with them are being ignored. These problems and issues will not go away.

Thanks and acknowledgements are due to: the co-op members who gave of their time and memories, and who by their purchase of shares in the Publishing Company helped to finance the writing of the book; the professionals and ex-professionals who kindly agreed to be interviewed; CDS, Wilkinson Hindle Halsall, Lloyd and Partners and Houghton and Stackpoole for their generous grants to the Publishing Company; Jules Lubbock; Joe Corbett, without whose persistence the book would never have been published; and Billy Floyd and Bill Halsall.

Further notes on how the co-op has been reported on, and how the book came to be written, are to be found in the Postscript. Readers who may at times be bewildered by the sequence of events are referred to the timetable of events at the end of the book.

I

Do You Get a Divi?:
The Roots of the Co-operative

Kate Kelly is a forceful woman with a boisterous sense of fun. Now in her mid-sixties, she lives with her daughter Kitty, Kitty's husband Danny, their children and Danny's birds in Sycamore Court. Some people jokingly refer to their house as 'the palace': it's immaculately furnished, immaculately kept.

Kate's a joker herself; a joker who'll take on anybody. She says of herself, 'I was the soft one. When they knew I'd get dressed up, they'd get dressed up too. I just feel I'm in charge of the co-op – I mean, the fund-raising part of it.' At one fund-raising do Lily Faulkner, one of the same generation, recalls Kate going up to 'that Chief Superintendent. Kate was dressed as one of those Eastern girls, with her bare midriff. And she went Oom, Oom, Oom, at him. And he took on this fit of laughing.'

At all-women coffee mornings (which serve only tea, in the afternoons) Kate's the bingo caller. She punctuates the numbers with racy jokes, mostly directed at the men. She's one of the women that make Tom Phillips, the co-op's clerk of works and friend, say: 'The language: they all use it. Somehow to me it sounds worse when the men say it. They just use it for the sake of using it. But the women – it seems natural to them somehow.'

Kate recalls when she first got a house of her own in the old Weller Streets area: 'In 1939 I went to live in Pecksniff Street. My sister-in-law lived there and she got me the house next door... You used to have to fight to get one of them houses. "Doll's houses" they used to call them. In one street you'd have about ten landlords. Y'ad to have your ten pound, key money. Anyway I was lucky, I got the house. It was nine shillings ten pence a week.'

You needed a friend, or more likely a relative, to get you a tenancy in those days in the area – Pecksniff, Micawber, Copperfield, Morton, Nickleby and Weller Streets. Although they were small, the houses were popular. To have a house at all was a step up from the flats and tenements in much of central Liverpool. Ivy Stead, another of Kate's generation, recalls feeling houseproud: 'You'd get down and scrub your step and – my husband was born in that house. I used to think, oh, isn't it posh up here? Most of the houses used to be painted the same. We'd pay a couple of fellers to do the whole street.'

Presumably it was the landlords who originally painted all the houses the same. But in many people's memories the same things are connected as Ivy connects: feeling houseproud; a sense of neighbourliness; and the houses being painted the same. Edie McLennan recalls of the same era: 'The back entries, as poor as people were, the gulleys were as clean as – people used to wash out the back themselves... You'd get the same coloured paint and anything you had over you'd pass on to people who didn't have a job, so they could do their own.'

The shared experience of poverty helped to bind people together, but also to fight one another. Sammy Roberts, now in his sixties, recalls in his childhood: 'I seen myself, my own mates, a crust of bread, I've seen them actually pinch it out of my hand. They couldn't afford apples at two for a penny. 'Cause I had twopence, threepence, fourpence I was the richest feller in the street: so I was a popular guy, like.'

Sammy was one of a large family. As he remembers his education: 'In them days they learnt you your ABC, how to count, how to work – and religion, to make you bitter.' Religion too both bound people together and divided them.

The area, before the Second World War, was on the border between Orange and Catholics, just within the Orange area. Ada Hewitt, now in her seventies, recalls:

'I remember my wedding went on for a week. Y'had the accordions out and the flags out and we'd be dancing in the street: real dancing...Like the 12th of July would go on for a fortnight. Every house would be decorated. There'd be riots then, they [Catholics] 'd have pepper thrown in their faces. I once went down with my sister on the 12th of July 'cause she had a verucca on her foot; then we couldn't get back, there was a line of police across our street.'

Sammy Roberts was from a strongly religious family. 'I used to live in an Orange area. It was very bitter before the war, you'd come out and defend the church...I had this mate, I was twelve before his mother let me in. When I went out, I'd left my cap. I went back and she was blessing where I'd sat with holy water – 'cause I was a Protestant coming to her house...A Catholic couldn't live in a Protestant street. They'd get hounded out. The landlords got to know...'

Other people have milder memories of the religious divisions. Lily Faulkner says, 'It was only when we were kids, they used to say it was I or O. On St Patrick's day you had to be I; on the 12th of July you had to be O.' Another expression was 'chips or peas?', peas being green. Joe McLennan, living on the border, says, 'There wasn't any trouble round our area. It'd be more jokative than anything. You always either drank together or worked together.'

The Second World War was a decisive turning-point: nearly everyone remembers some change dating from then. The wartime itself left a majority of women in the area to endure the bombing and the shortages. It helped to reinforce the mutual help between neighbours. Ivy Stead: 'I went to hospital to have a thyroid done. The lady next door took mine in, 'cause I couldn't get my husband home, he was in the army.'

Hilda Mills was a lifelong resident in the area. 'I lived in Pecksniff Street. I'd lived there since 1934. I was born in 58 Micawber Street: my mother and father had been there since they were married...Then I went down on the Munitions 'cause I was a widow at twenty-three. The neighbours used to look after our two.'

The end of the war brought the establishment of the welfare state and the National Health Service, the end of the times when, as Ivy Stead puts it, 'An ordinary woman 'd go across and deliver a baby.' Sammy Roberts remembers his return home as being a decisive turning-point in his attitude to religion: 'When I came home my mother said to me, "What?" she said, "get out of this house." 'Cause I said, "I've been out there six and a half years. There's no such thing as a Catholic man and a Protestant man: we all fought together." Now I've had children: some have married Catholics and some have married Protestants.'

Old prejudices began to break down. Post-war housing programmes put Catholics and Protestants together willy-nilly. But at the same time post-war affluence brought new values to the area, eroding some of the old community spirit. Joe McLennan says, 'Before the war it used to be all old neighbours. Time went on, old neighbours started leaving the district. New neighbours came in: more toffee-nosed...At the top end they used to have a party in the street, but at the bottom end, I don't know if they thought they were a bit more snobbish...These new neighbours came in and wanted to paint [the houses] different colours.'

There were big street parties for weddings, and for events like the Coronation. Women like Kate Kelly would whip up support and organize things. But the houses themselves began to deteriorate, as Kate recounts: 'It got dilapidated 'cause the landlord wouldn't do any repairs. The houses started to sink. We had a lot of bombing in the war and that got at the foundations. From the wartime they went down the nick.'

Kate remembers the post-war improvements to the houses as a mixed blessing: 'We got electric put in. The first night we put the electric on we heard this scratching. He was prising this wood off under the stairs. Lo and behold, there was millions and millions of cockroaches. We'd never noticed before, 'cause we only had gas. He'd get a blowlamp and say, "Put the light on."'

Kate decided to give the Public Health a little present. 'I took this box [of them] down to the Corporation. The feller said, "What's this?" "If they're not claimed in three months they're your own," I said to him.'

The houses had always been small. When they were built in the 1860s, they were the smallest houses built under the then local by-laws. A century or so later they'd come to seem very small indeed. Sammy Roberts says, 'We were a family of thirteen and we lived in a house with an outside toilet and only two bedrooms...We even had to split up our meals. All the elderly 'd eat first and the rest of us 'd sit on the stairs watching them.'

The Robertses were an exceptionally large family; but even for an ordinary-sized one, it was crowded, and a tremendous job to keep the place in any kind of order. Kate says, 'We had no bathroom. We had a shed built on for a back kitchen. We had a tin bath: me, my husband and three kids had the same bath. I remember one Christmas, I'd been stripped naked in the bath basting the turkey in the oven; and while I've been basting the turkey the dog jumped in the bath.'

For the generation born during or just after the war, these were the conditions they grew up in; these were the memories they grew up with. 'Years ago families stuck by one another': a lot of them say that, or something similar. By the time they were setting up home for themselves you could still get a tenancy by being known to the landlord, even though a lot of the smaller landlords had been bought out by then.

So, for example, when Ivy Stead's son John married Irene,

25

and when Kitty,* Kate's daughter, married Danny Heague (Kitty and Irene becoming sisters-in-law by marriage in the process), they got a house in the area. Many of the younger people preferred their first home to be a terraced house in familiar surroundings, bathroom or no bathroom, rather than a Corpie flat or maisonette.

Kate herself, though, fed up with the conditions, had moved out in the early 1960s: 'I'd been on the Corporation housing list for nineteen years. Eventually I got a Group A card and they offered me a maisonette in Halewood. I'd waited that long I took it.' But after a few years on the outlying estate, 'I came back to Kitty to stay for a fortnight; and I'm still here fourteen years later.' Everyone, by the 1970s, had a relative or friend who'd been through the same experience: of moving to an outlying estate, and feeling less happy there.

Nevertheless the younger generation found conditions hard to tolerate. Overcrowding that their parents had struggled to cope with seemed increasingly unfair as the general standard of living improved all around them. Kitty recalls: 'When I lived in Micawber Street there were seven of us in two bedrooms. It ended up with four of them and my mother in the same bed, 'cause she told 'em ghost stories and they wouldn't get back in their own beds.' It made her angry: 'There was something on the telly about a man on the moon. And there was us with a toilet in the backyard. I was determined my kids wouldn't have to do what I did: sleeping in the same bed with my two brothers when I was fifteen, and taking the bucket up to bed.'

Washing machines, fridges and televisions had arrived in many houses by now, and somehow space was found for them.

---

*Women brought up in the area are known there by their maiden names: Kitty as Kitty Kelly not Heague, Ann Caddis (married name Rice), Thelma Rath (married name Floyd). But people'd say to me: 'Kitty Kelly: you'll know her as Kitty Heague.' So I've used the names outsiders are expected to use: the married ones.

Yet they seemed out of place. Liz Dono, born just after the war, has moved out of the area now: 'Where I am now, the girls look at my photos and say, "What's that next to the gas fire?" And I say, "It's the fridge-freezer. There was nowhere else to put it."' The houses themselves seemed out of place in the modern world. Liz's husband Harry says of the 1970s: 'People like in the bookie's 'd say, "Remember the days when we used to go down the back" – and we were still going down the back. And "Remember the old tin bath" – and I'd say, "Come home, we'll boil up a bit of water." We used to empty it out of the washing machine into the bath.'

Some of the old spirit of the area remained, though. Kate recalls how she had always used to organize 'parties, anything involving the children. Then Kitty took over as she got older. There was never any problem getting a chara together.' Kitty says, 'That part of the Weller Streets has always been there': there largely through the efforts of Kitty and one or two others.

Sammy Roberts says it wasn't quite 'community' spirit: 'We were neighbours, we all knew one another, helped out if you were sick...You were acknowledged wherever you went. You knew by lips, you know, what was happening.'

But the houses themselves were deteriorating even further. By the mid-1970s owners couldn't get an improvement grant because the houses had a limited life. Landlords did few repairs. Yet no one seemed to know when clearance would happen either. There was a general feeling of powerlessness about the housing conditions.

In contrast, there'd been considerable changes in the post-war period where people worked. Wages had increased; and through the unions working people had established some collective power. Sammy Roberts describes the changes he saw in his working life as a docker: 'The only way you could get on the dock was if your father was a docker...They started bringing other lads in 'cause they were losing their jobs as brickies or whatever. Then we got a nucleus of people who wanted to work and were a bit more educated than our fathers were. And they started negotiations, the shop stewards. Once, *they* wouldn't let us up the stairs. Then *they* seen: they're not Communists, they're elected. We started getting round a table.'

Sammy himself had been a moderate, anti-Communist shop-steward for some years. 'I'm there for peace if you can get it. If you can't get it, you fight.' By the mid-1970s the power the unions had established began to weaken in the face of mechanization and recession.

But people in the Weller Streets area had never felt the kind of collective power unions had learnt to wield, as far as their housing was concerned. If you couldn't afford to buy your own home, you either rented on the shrinking private market, or you took your chances with the – remote – Corporation.

There'd been an action group, off and on, since the mid-1960s. Kitty and a few other women of her generation, Kate and a few of hers, would get together and get a petition signed, have a march. It got nowhere. The men, if they were active at all, would confine their politics to the workplace, or political parties, or discussions in the pub. Action groups were 'talking shops': the men skitted the women for bothering. Billy Floyd, one of the post-war generation, says, 'I was interested in politics but I never joined any of the parties or anything. And that was it until I met Kevin... Up and down the alehouses in Park Road that was what we used to talk about, politics. I think it used to bore the tarts. They were talking about nappies and we were talking about Mao Tse Tung.'

The conditions of the houses would come home to the men, though, after a night out on the ale. Thelma Floyd remembers how Billy 'fell down one night and ended up at the bottom of the stairs with the bath on his back like a tortoise'. It wasn't that the men weren't concerned, in a general way, about the area's decline. They just didn't see what could be done.

Stephen Rice, the same age as Billy, says, 'There was that undercurrent that had been there a long time before it took: the undercurrent of discontent with the conditions. My mother once said to me. "By the time you leave school we'll be in a nice new home." By the time I was thirty we were still on the same street.'

Individually many of the women had tried to improve their family's situation by applying to the Corpie for rehousing. Kitty says, 'I'd been on the Corpie list for seventeen years. With my mother and the kids in a two-up two-down. I had twenty-five points but I still couldn't be rehoused.'

Kitty could, after a while, have been rehoused; but only on an outlying estate like the one her mother had already returned from. Ann Byrne, married to the 'Kevin' Billy Floyd mentions, had less chance: 'I was on the list for ten years and had seven and a half points with three children. I went down to say, can I have one of these 3,000 empty houses. And the feller said, "I've got four keys, you can have any one of them." They were the hard-to-lets.'

One of the angriest about her treatment by the Corporation was Ann Caddis, Stephen Rice's older sister: 'I had a girl and two boys sleeping in the same room with me. They offered me a flat in Belle Vale – they're all getting pulled down now – and I said, "No thanks, I'll stay in the slum where I am." And d'you know what they said to me? They said, "You'll only get rehoused if you get cancer." And twelve months later I was in Clatterbridge with cancer of the womb. That's what's made me bitter about the Corporation.'

Some people accepted what the Corpie offered. Those who remained began to realize that their best hope lay in getting something done about their present housing: short-term repairs, long-term rehousing. Everyone accepted the houses couldn't now be improved to a decent long-term standard. In the early 1970s there'd been a brief flurry of hope that some repairs would get done. Realmdeal Properties by then owned over half the houses: 'I tell you what got the action group going. They were going to rehab them; then the Receiver got involved. We were left up in the air, we couldn't get no joy at all. It was the not knowing.'

This is Stephen Cossack talking, another of the immediate post-war generation – the only man prepared to cross the sexual divide and work with the women in an action group. He got particularly involved when, in 1975, the properties of the bankrupt Realmdeal were taken over by CDS, a London-based housing association. At first they did the management from London. A short-term repairs programme, involving patch-repairing of the houses and the installation of hot-water geysers, got under way.

But because of the distance from London, and incompetent organization, the repair programme went badly. Steve Cossack says, 'We were getting a lot of sympathy and nothing from CDS. It came as a bit of a shock to us. We'd never had anything to do with the machinations of bureaucracy.' Soon CDS London opened a local office, but it was too late to get a grip on the repairs programme.

So the action group, including Steve Cossack, Kitty Heague, Irene Stead, Ann Caddis, Ann Byrne, got together. The Corporation had, in 1976, a list of fifty-seven clearance areas – the fifty-seven varieties, somebody called them – and the Weller Streets was at the bottom. The action group put round a petition for quicker clearance. Irene says, 'We had no go in us. We used to just go and listen to councillors. No one took notes or anything.'

But they organized a protest march to the Town Hall. Irene says Ann Caddis, the spokeswoman, 'got a big applause that day. The girl that ran the Merlin Street [Community Centre] minded all the babies 'cause I think it began at eleven. We all carried umbrellas with holes in and a tin bath. They wouldn't let us walk on the road. I don't think they let us take the bath in.'

Ann Caddis recalls: 'When we tried to get the houses pulled down, they said it would be about ten years. We said, we can't wait ten years. So we got a petition up. I was the speaker. We done a protest march from our houses to the Town Hall. We lobbied them outside, then we had five minutes to speak. All the councillors were there. Oh, they clapped and that, but that was it.'

It was a cheerful yet dispiriting occasion. 'They' – the police who wouldn't let the women walk on the road, the officials who wouldn't let them take the bath in, the councillors who clapped – were polite, and vaguely sympathetic, and then got on with their other business.

In fact the protest had coincided with the Council considering a comprehensive policy for the renewal of older housing. So, by the winter of 1976/7 it was proposed that the Weller Streets be cleared by 1981. People had heard promises like that before. And where, even if it were true, would people be rehoused? As Steve Cossack says, 'The action group came to life with rumours . . . It started through talking really and everyone was irate about it: spontaneous anger.'

This was the network of neighbours where, in Sammy Roberts' phrase, 'you knew by lips' what was going on. Steve goes on: 'The set-up was the street, where everybody chatted. The rumour was – with foundation as it happened – there were 3,000 vacant properties and that was what we were going to get a choice of. And they were suspected of being hard-to-let. We were asking questions of where they were.'

People in the action group had got to know one or two of the local workers for CDS. One of them, Sue Jackson, helped to set up a meeting with the Council official responsible for clearance and new building. Ann Byrne and Ann Caddis went along, with Sue. As they reported back, he said: 'At the moment there are no sites available in the Liverpool 8 area for building houses. This means that when the houses are knocked down it will not be possible for residents to be rehoused locally.'

Sue Jackson's record of the meeting says that 'This reply produced even greater demoralization than the 1981 deadline [for clearance] since that deadline is meaningless or simply frightening if there is nowhere for tenants to go.' In addition she records that the Council official 'was astonished that no one expressed any interest in compensation and was suitably silent when the tenants told him they weren't interested in money, they want houses'.

The Liverpool branch of CDS was at this time in the process of breaking away from its London head office. In April 1977 it became a separate Liverpool-based organization, interested in involving tenants in housing management and in housing co-operatives. So in early 1977 the members of the action group who were CDS tenants – the majority – began to put their efforts into 'Dickens Co-op'. Steve and his wife Cathy, Kitty, Ann Caddis and Ann Byrne and a few others would meet in Steve's house or CDS's office at 38 Geraint Street.

Nobody was very clear what 'co-op' meant to people living in a proposed clearance area. There were already a number of housing co-ops in Liverpool, but they were doing improvement and conversion of older housing. Improvement and conversion didn't apply to the 'Dickens' area. Catherine Meredith, the Director of CDS, says, 'It was a pretty pathetic situation, 'cause they were clearance, and we really had nothing to offer them... What we were hoping was, they would manage the decline of their area into clearance.'

Nobody was interested in that. But they all learnt something about co-ops. Steve Cossack was interested in Labour politics, and had been involved in the union at Ford's. He got intrigued. 'I used to spend a lot of time with Kevin Morris [of CDS]. He talked to me about co-operative principles, the ins and outs of it. I was impressed by it.' Everyone had an equal, pound share in the running of a 'par value' co-operative; everyone had an equal say; everyone had an equal benefit. 'I used to go every single day, just chatting,' Steve says.

But he and the others weren't interested in the idea of managing the decline of the area. They were looking for a way of getting decent rehousing. Steve: 'Then somebody said, how about new-build? There was a green National Federation of Housing Associations' booklet . . . The idea was first mooted in private conversations with CDS workers. But the first time I thought about it really seriously was reading that booklet.'

Steve says he lent the booklet to Ann Byrne and never got it back. She and others on the action group were vaguely interested in the idea; he began to feel more strongly than that. He used to go for a pint in Wilkie's* on Park Road, and he started chatting about it in there. One person he met in the pub around this time was Rory Heap, a blind man of about Steve's age. Rory was a community worker for the local Toxteth Community Council. Rory recalls conversations in the pub: 'Steve Cossack said we need a new approach. It was all a bit vague. People were saying, "We're going to have to do something different if we're going to get taken any notice of." CDS were involved, and Sue Jackson, because they had a number of tenants. CDS started coming on with "Why don't they form a co-operative?" People were saying, "What the fuck's a co-operative?" And I was very suspicious: I mean, they were landlords.'

The women on the action group were suspicious of CDS as landlords too. But they'd quickly come to trust Sue Jackson, then in her early twenties: a woman clearly from a different, middle-class background, but open and friendly. Rory himself says, 'Sue Jackson turned out to be very straight.' Sue and her co-worker Kevin Morris helped to organize a survey. Ann Caddis remembers this as a direct result of the demoralizing meeting with the Council official in January: 'Me and Ann Byrne and Sue Jackson went down and had a confab with him

---

*Wilkie's is the Crown on Park Road, known by the name of a former publican, as are most of the local pubs. Others call it Maggie's.

and an argument with him and got nothing. So we decided to do a survey to see who wanted to form a co-operative. We had a rep on each street.'

Steve felt the action group's lobbying had only resulted in vague promises and a bit of publicity. 'We'd exhausted every angle by non-political means, we were fed up with getting photographed in our pits... It was in our house after the woman from the *Weekly News* had come. We started chatting about it.'

Steve says, 'We went round with a questionnaire... That was quietly organized by Sue Jackson and Kevin Morris, and we did it. We gave it to CDS and they did statistical work on it. We were just asking them, finding out what the needs of the area were.'

Interest was uncertain. People vaguely understood that the idea of a co-op was to get a site and build houses on it. The result of the questionnaire was 'Everybody wanted Aigburth'. Aigburth was a popular residential area two miles further out. But nobody knew whether it was a real possibility; nor whether it was possible to get a site, or the government money to pay for the building.

Steve wanted to push the idea further though. 'We decided we'd put it to the residents that we could possibly form a co-operative... We thought if we could get the backing we could do it. So we leafleted the area and put notices in all the shops, then a week later we leafleted again.'

About fifty people came to that first meeting in June 1977, in the big class-like room in Merlin Street Community Centre. The hard core of the old action group came: Steve and Cathy, Kitty, Irene, the two Anns amongst them. Ann Byrne persuaded Kevin to come; Ann Caddis persuaded her husband Alec. Others had their interest sparked off by the leaflets and the general chat in the street and the pub. Here's Ann Caddis talking to Billy Floyd: 'Curiosity, that's what got you involved, isn't it? 'cause Thelma said to me, "What's all this about?" And I said, Why don't you come along to the meeting?'

Billy, like some of the other men, came under pressure from two sides. Thelma said to him, 'Come on, you're always talking about politics, why not do something?' And in the pub Steve Cossack talked about it. Billy: 'I remember there was a group of us, it was about quarter to eleven, in the alehouse. And we said, "Why don't we go along?" So [the next day] I went, just to go along to heckle, like.'

Rory Heap, the community worker, had given Steve some advice on tactics for the meeting. So it began with a question and answer session with Alec Doswell – a local Labour councillor, and Steve's uncle – before the co-op came up. Steve recalls: 'It was Heaps's idea, that, to have Doswell there. To demand answers from him. So he in effect became a foil for the idea of a co-op. Because he didn't have any answers, you see.'

Sue Jackson recalls the mood, and Steve's role at this stage: 'I remember – there was quite a lot of reluctance and – it wasn't exactly something they could walk into easily. Steve was a most strongly motivating force. I . . . felt that was because he was quite politically aware, because of his experience at Ford's. He had learnt about power and control, and that it was more accessible than people in the Weller Streets themselves thought.'

Steve saw the co-op as a way of bringing the 'power and control' people had in their workplace to bear on their housing. But at that first meeting he didn't put it across very well. 'I made the tragic mistake of trying to put six months of chatting into less than an hour. It came out as gibberish.'

It was a chaotic meeting. Fifty people were more than the action group had been used to. Billy Floyd says, 'One bloke stood up and said, "What's it mean, then? This co-op? Do you get a divi?"* And somebody else stood up and said, "Ah shut up, you're a divvy yourself," and everybody laughed.'

---

*'Divi' is the dividend you used to get in Co-op retail shops; 'divvy' is Scouse for 'idiot'.

Everybody laughed, but it was a serious point. The only 'co-op' most people knew of was the Co-op shop, where you did get a divi. Steve tried to explain it wasn't that kind of co-op, when somebody else stood up: a staunch, long-standing member of the action group known to the others as 'Jaws'. Kitty recalls her as someone who 'used to go and sit in the Town Hall every week just to listen'. At the meeting she took a stand on principle: '"Why should we build our own frigging houses?" she said, and her teeth fell out – that's why we called her Jaws. She wouldn't get involved and took about twenty people with her. She said, "You're all fools. Somebody else is getting paid to do what you're doing."'

Despite the confusion, Billy recalls the basic message as coming across: 'Steve said, "We can either go on doing what we have been doing: having petitions, lobbying councillors. And we all know where that's got us. Or we can do nothing and let 'em walk all over us. Or we can form a co-op." That's how he put it. The choice, like.'

But nobody could come to any coherent conclusion. Then Steve recounts, 'It was a spontaneous reaction from the floor. Somebody said, "Why don't we look into it?" So we formed a working party.'

The meeting broke up, having agreed to form a working party from volunteers at the meeting. Steve, Kitty, Irene and Ann Byrne remained from the old action group. Among the new recruits were Billy Floyd and three others of the same generation, in their late twenties or early thirties: Eifion Wynn-Jones, an office manager, Harry Dono who worked as a taxi driver, and Billy Odger who worked in Ford's. There were also two young women, who, Billy Floyd says, were 'trainee teachers at the time. They got used: 'cause they were bright they were coerced on to the working party.'

Billy Floyd says that at the working party 'Sue was making the running...She sort of chaired those meetings.' They met in a room in CDS's office in Geraint Street, a temporarily converted terraced house. They sat among the desks and files and CDS paperwork, talking to people Sue Jackson and Rory Heap invited along. 'The idea', Billy recalls, 'was to have a different thing each week. I think we had a couple of tame architects. We had Lawrence Holden.' He was CDS's solicitor, and talked about the legal side of co-ops.

The working party also began to consider where they might be able to build. 'Rory got this surveyor. He was getting fucking survey maps. "There's stuff not on these maps," he was saying. "There's loads of land up there that's not marked."'

Their main work, though, involved catching up with what Steve Cossack had already latched on to about co-ops: that a new-build co-operative could provide decent rehousing for people as a community, controlled by the community, paid for by the government. Billy Odger says, 'It all seemed good when Adrian Moran [of CDS] and Sue Jackson started explaining. 'Cause none of us had any experience of going after a site, forming a committee.'

At this time, in mid-1977, there was only a handful of new-build housing co-operatives in Britain. These were either for the relatively well-off (co-ownership societies), and were built before residents were known, or were for students and young people in London. Legally they were 'housing associations'; non-profit-making bodies, mainly funded and supervised by the Housing Corporation, a government body with regional offices, including one in Liverpool.

So much the working party learned. 'Most of it was yapping about how to organize,' as Billy Floyd puts it. There was a bit of a clash between the two 'trainee teachers' and the rest of the working party. 'You're talking about a load of scallies* you know,' Billy says. 'I remember saying to those girls, at least

---

* 'Scallies': scallywags, rascals: a Scouse way of praising yourself with faint damnation.

we're learning something. They turned to me, as if to say, Ha ha, fucking divvy.'

Steve says of the majority of the working party, 'We reached the conclusion that we could form a co-op with five years' hard graft involved.' Billy says of the two young women's reaction to that: 'They disappeared. They reached the conclusions but didn't relish the work.' Kitty says there was another reason: 'Those two girls didn't think people like you could do it.'

Nobody had done it before. None of the people involved had much experience of meetings, politics, building, anything relevant. It was a crazy conclusion to come to. Steve Cossack recalls how another local Labour councillor echoed that view when the working party told people they wanted to go ahead. 'When the working party reported back to the public meeting and said we could do it, Taylor said, "You're offering these people dreams. These pensioners deserve more than this."'

The last meeting of the working party had decided Billy Floyd should chair that first public meeting. Irene Stead says, 'Billy Floyd was picked 'cause he was the milkman of the area: he could pass messages on.' He himself says, 'We decided in Geraint Street that I had the biggest mouth. I understood the people in the area better than most. I was going to be the foil at that first meeting with the others making studied comments.'

The main 'studied comments' were to come from Steve Cossack. 'I said, "This is the result of the working party. We say go: if we've got your support, like." And they all fucking mumbled. So, looking for something to get it going, we said, "We've got to give ourselves a name." And there were all these weird and wonderful names. Then this voice from the back says, "We can call it Sussex Effing Gardens* for all I care, just get on with it."'

The name was the biggest item of discussion at that meeting.

---

*The name of the local office of the housing department. The 'Effing' doesn't usually appear on the board outside.

'We decided', Steve says, 'on Weller Street: the one that bisected the others.' Most people remembered, as Billy did, 'When I was a kid, saying that was where I was going. It was the street with no houses on, where you'd go. "I'm just off to Weller Street," you'd say.'

Many people were pretty dubious about the idea of the co-op. 'I wasn't keen on the idea,' Rozzie Lybert, Kitty's aunt, says, 'I thought it was pie in the sky. I thought it was a crazy idea.' Nevertheless, pushed by the enthusiasm of Steve Cossack and Billy Floyd, backed by the quieter support of the rest of the working party, the public meeting decided in principle to launch the Weller Streets Housing Co-operative. The working party was to form the nucleus of a Steering Committee with Billy in the chair. He'd proved unexpectedly good at directing the meeting, with a mixture of shouting at people and cracking jokes. Ivy Stead says of him: 'He is brainy. Billy's got more of a punch behind him. He was a case as well, like.'

The local county councillor, Margaret Simey, had also been at the meeting. 'Let me know if you need any help,' she'd said to Billy in her posh voice at the beginning. And at the end: 'There you are, you didn't need my help, did you?'

Rory Heap says: 'The curious thing about early enthusiasm was, it was based upon vision and anger, not on any rigorous sense of what might happen.' The experiences of past generations, and the frustration of previous efforts to do something about the housing conditions in the area, came together. Ann Byrne says, 'It was anger for us. We just wanted to smack 'em, to put one over on *them*, like.' Steve Cossack says that what drew him to the co-op idea was 'the idea of beating the pigs at their own game. These so-and-so's have put me in an unenviable position. I want to say, "You've put me in a pit and I've climbed out of it myself."'

For the women, though, there was often more of an emphasis on getting rehoused. Kitty says: 'To us, we wanted a better house for us and our kids.' The practical necessity of getting something done about their housing backed the urge for a fight, and the idealism of believing in the community and wanting it to stay together. Stephen Rice comments: 'The lack of action by the Council fostered this kind of kamikaze attitude that we've got nothing, so we've got nothing to lose. It's a nice attitude in that you can take anybody on.'

In contrast to the old action group with its overwhelming majority of women, the steering committee, as it established itself over its first few meetings, had a majority of men. Steve Cossack says the other men, in the action group days, 'thought we were just wasting our time'. He says, 'I think there was the traditional thing, the men's role was the heavy political one. It was below the dignity of the men, to work with the women.'

Kitty and Irene Stead have remained on the committee of the co-op since that first meeting. Kitty says, 'The women dwindled away. They put it to us at the beginning it'd be four or five meetings a week and the men had more time...I was one of the lucky ones. I had my mum living with me to cook the tea and look after the kids.'

The co-op idea moved people's concern about housing from the traditional province of the women – domestic, based on the street – to the traditional province of the men – politics, evening meetings, discussions in the pub. The men were more attracted to the 'fight'; the women to bettering their housing conditions. Billy Floyd, who when asked why he got involved in the co-op says, 'I wanted to connive', buttonholed other men he knew. So Kevin Byrne became more deeply involved than Ann, though she continued to have an active role; Alec Caddis became more active than his wife Ann. Billy also, for instance, approached John Stead, whose mother Ivy recalls: 'Our John and Billy Floyd knew one another when they were so high. They used to do windows on Sundays, then I'd make them bacon and eggs.' John wasn't interested; his wife Irene stayed on the committee with Kitty.

But both elements were crucial to how the co-op developed: the men's role, and the women's. Sue Jackson says Billy 'tackled the intellectual questions of what being a co-op meant – which Kitty, however forceful, never felt. She was very much one for mustering the troops, trying to make sure people pulled their weight.' That was certainly the men's view. In practice Kitty and Irene had one of the most difficult roles of all: to work as partners with the male majority of the committee, while acting as arbiters when opinions divided on sexual lines. Men were either the co-op's leaders, or stayed well in the background; while the women's social network and their determination to get their families into decent homes – reflected in their being consistently in the majority at meetings – underpinned everything that was to come.

2

Beware Your New-found Friends:
Politics and the Search for Land

Many people think of Billy Floyd as – like Kate Kelly – a joker: a joker who'll take on anybody. Kitty says, 'It's just his way: the type of feller you don't know which way to take. I think he's always been clever.' But his cleverness had always had a dissenting streak in it. He himself says, 'I was always a fucking big mouth at school. If I had a...grievance I'd stand up for myself.' He'd stand up for himself, though, only half-seriously. Others knew him more for the way he'd take the piss out of everything with a joke.

He'd always been interested in politics in a vaguely socialist sort of way, without ever belonging to any party. His only experience of political action had been in the early 1960s, as a teenager, when he'd been an engineering apprentice. 'Apprenticeship then, the rates of pay – it's probably better now, but then, you were virtually paying them to do it, like...It wouldn't have been so bad if we were just learning, but we were actually having to do full-rate jobs...So I got talking to the other lads about what we were getting.'

He'd tried, then, the established way; of going through the union. 'They couldn't do anything. You were indentured to the company, you were just an associate member of the union. That wasn't good enough for me. So we used to meet in the Clock in London Road. It was like our own union. We got some of the lads in from other companies.'

An unsuccessful strike had followed. 'I was one of the last

two back. We got a rousing reception off the shop floor. But we got fucking dressed down – told we were Trotskyite Reds and all that.'

Maybe it was just coincidence, but the idea of the co-op was similar in many ways to Billy's teenage experience. It grew from a long-standing sense of grievance; there wasn't any established way of getting together to do something about the grievance; so people got together to create something new, 'like our own union'.

Certainly Billy got hold of the co-op idea as strongly and as quickly as Steve Cossack had done. 'From the first few meetings I knew it could be done.' While the working party had been looking at the problems, Billy says, 'The thing then was that it was fucking interesting, but it was good fun.' But as soon as the co-op began in earnest the 'fun' was harder to earn for Billy and some of the others. Here, for instance, is the agenda for the general meeting of 1 September 1977:

1. Minutes of the last meeting – are they correct?
2. Membership – who can be a member?
3. Rules – which ones to choose for registering?
4. Site – which land to try and buy?
5. The Agreement with CDS.
6. Finance – how to raise money?
7. Education Programme – how to organize it?
8. Any Other Business.
9. Next Meeting.

This is only one month after the public meeting that had resolved to form a co-op. Within a very short space of time, the 'crazy idea' had turned into a bloody complicated business, and Billy was at the middle of it. For a start they had to learn how to run meetings: the small committee meetings in CDS's Geraint Street office; the larger general ones, for everyone interested, in the Zion Chapel, a high, dingy square room on Northumberland Street.

Eifion Wynn-Jones says of early meetings: 'After a while, after people got to know the committee it was all done right – "Speak through the chair" – At the beginning it was, "Hey Billy that's a load of shite," and all that. Luckily we had a few people who'd been to union meetings so they knew the drill.'

But in fact most of the men with union or Labour Party experience were sitting cagily on the sidelines at first. Peter Tyrrell, for instance: 'It surprised me in the early days, to see how committed people really were. I was a convenor in fucking Lairds at one time and people who were losing their jobs weren't as committed as these people.'

'These people' – straight away there was a group of leaders, demonstrating how 'committed' they were to the others. Eifion says it was all done right 'after people got to know the committee'. The idea of a committee doing the donkey work took root from the outset, from the small group of people on the working party, and then the decision to endorse the working party's recommendation and form a Steering Committee. On that there were Billy and Steve, both committed to the 'fight'. There was Kitty, of whom Harry Dono says, 'Kitty, if anything's going to get done she seemed to be the one started the ball rolling.' There were Harry himself, Billy Odger, George Millington, Arthur Roberts: all steady men who were interested but not particularly experienced. Arthur Roberts says of Billy Odger: 'He seemed to have the same feelings as me. You think the same as these others but you're not as outgoing as these...madarses.' There were Ann Byrne and Irene Stead who'd stuck with it from the action group days. Irene, with experience of office work, had got pressed into being Secretary.

But, as Harry says, 'At the beginning there was a lot of people who were interested in it, but wouldn't put the footwork in.' And there was a lot of footwork to do. Hardly before they knew what they were doing, the committee had agreed to adopt a set of 'model rules' CDS and someone from the Housing Corporation's Co-operative Housing Agency had given them, and had applied for registration as an industrial and provident society – whatever that meant. Kitty says, 'The committee did take on a lot of responsibility. The seven people who signed when we got registered, we were all frightened, saying, "What've we signed?" We'll all be liable if anything goes wrong."'

While CDS people assured committee members they wouldn't be financially 'liable', they still felt morally 'liable', responsible to the others. They'd been working hard in the first few weeks to understand just what the important issues were: that agenda of 1 September summarizes them. Then they were trying to communicate what they'd learnt to general meetings. Steve says, 'We had public meetings every week which were to discuss what the working party had discussed. And we were getting eighty people turning out. The Labour Party would be glad of that many.'

It wasn't always eighty people, but it was weekly at first. Billy says, 'At the time we thought that'd keep people's attention. We were trying to get people to understand the mechanics: the minutes, Chairman, Secretary.' While the frequency was soon reduced, the style continued as it began. As Billy describes it: 'Early on we were trying so hard to look professional. We were trying to put on a front to our own people, saying to them, "You've been abandoned by the fucking system, your backs are against the wall."'

The 'front' at meetings was also a bit of a performance, to keep people's interest. Different speakers came. People came from the Housing Corporation and said government money might be available if the co-op could find a site, because the Housing Corporation was reserving up to 10 per cent of its funds for co-ops at the time. Adrian Moran and Sue Jackson came from CDS to start the 'education programme'. The committee used to sit at the front, showing their 'responsibility' and 'commitment': Irene for one remembers hating that.

Billy'd alternately harangue and joke at people, so that, as Kitty recalls, 'Some of the people'd go mad at him, shouting and swearing – but they'd still come back to the meeting next week.'

Eifion, with his office experience, had been pressed by Billy into the role of treasurer, and of Minutes Secretary if Irene couldn't come: 'Any clerical work that had to be done,' he says. 'I left the organizing to Billy and the others, and they could forget all about the paperwork.' Billy used Eifion's appearance as a bit of show business: 'At meetings I had him wheeled on to the front. I was using him: This is the civilized bit, I mean he's got fucking brains, he wears a suit and tie. He wasn't like the rest of the riff-raff – I think he often brought a briefcase.'

But the work of the early days – August/September 1977 – wasn't just meetings. For active committee members they were the tip of the iceberg. The nine-tenths not showing to the public meetings was the graft involved in those items on that 1 September agenda. 'Which land to try and buy?' was clearly the priority. They followed up the advice of the 'tame surveyor' who'd been to the working party, by going out to look at the land they'd identified on maps. Steve recalls how they did that: 'We did our own survey. We all piled into cars and taxis. We measured the land by sight. Stumbled across all sorts of weird and wonderful things, like site-boring where nobody was supposed to be. We ran across a government storage depot which nobody knew was there...and a dairy farm – in the middle of Liverpool!'

Harry Dono got involved in this because, as Billy says, 'We used the cab a lot for reconnoitring.' Irene Stead recalls: 'If Harry Dono said he didn't have any fares, say Wednesday afternoon, we'd all go out. We'd just get out and look at any bit of land.'

When they could get off work Irene and Kitty would join Billy, Steve and Harry on the search for land. Kitty recalls:

'You'd go on the search for land and put the dinner on, and you came back so late the dinner's all burnt.' And it was harder for the women in more ways than one: 'Whenever the taxi passed a copper they all had to get down, and Irene said she always landed up at the bottom.' From early on Kitty and Irene got used to taking a fair amount of horse-play and joking around at their expense from the male majority.

The search for land made people optimistic: there seemed to be a lot of potential sites, ranging from the enormous site of the defunct Dingle Oil Terminal, to a little site everyone liked opposite Sefton Park, on the edge of Aigburth. At the same time the search for ways of raising money led to more work for committee members. Harry Dono had once worked for a paper manufacturer's, and suggested they collect waste paper: 'We knocked on people's doors, said would they leave it and we'd collect it.' Harry in his cab, Alec Caddis in his van, would go up and down the streets doing the collecting. Alec: 'There must've been people thought we were idiots. Kids used to chase us, throwing papers in the back.'

Alec's wife Ann thinks the 'paper chase' helped, early on, to get the less interested people involved. 'It got people going, just in doing that. "Come and get mine, they've been there three weeks," they'd say.' There were rumours that one or two newsagents opened their doors in the morning to find their usual supply of papers missing. And somebody mentioned that soaking the paper in water made it weigh more, so you'd get a bit more money for it.

Meanwhile a group of the women collected rags. Kitty says, 'There was me, Ann Byrne, Thelma [Floyd], Irene, we used to take the rags back on a Wednesday afternoon then go in the Globe for a glass of lager.'

'The set-up was the street, where everybody chatted.' People started talking about the co-op. Harry: 'You get the likes of old people who knew everyone. They'd start talking in the shop, and somebody'd say, "What's this co-op?"' Peter

Tyrrell says, 'I got to know of it 'cause of people talking about it or coming round the doors.'

Many people still know of Billy Floyd as 'Billy the bottle'. He was on the doorstep every day, pushing the newspapers out of his way so he could deliver the milk. Eifion says, 'Billy's round'd be taking twice as long 'cause of people asking him questions.' Harry remembers, 'If you wanted to know anything, all you had to do was get up in the morning and talk to the milkman.'

Kitty, Irene and Steve were the other main ones who'd go knocking on doors to talk about the co-op. Lily Faulkner, for instance, recalls: 'Irene Stead came down. I was out at the time. The woman opposite said she'd been. I got hold of Billy in the morning. He said, "OK, Lil, write a letter in saying can you join."' And Billy Lybert, a cousin to the Kelly's, says, 'We got shanghaied into it. Y'know, Kitty said, "Come on, get down there." So we went to the meetings in the Zion Chapel. At first it seemed a lot of rubbish.'

Nevertheless, he kept coming. What was there to lose? If this crazy idea came off, your attendance at meetings would put you in line for a house. If it failed, you'd got out of the house for a few nights. Billy Odger says: 'I'd just have been sitting at home watching the telly. It got me out.' As one of the quieter committee members, he says, 'I thought it went reasonably smoothly myself. Y'ad the questions thrown at you. It was new to me till I got involved. When you started to explain to people, how it was trying to get the money out of the government to get a site off the Council to build the houses – then they understood.'

Committee members explained it as they understood it. Billy Odger's view was one everyone could relate to. But behind his view was a more complicated problem: what the 'trying' involved was working out how to get a site off the Council. The search for land had shown there were sites around; but the co-op had to move on from identifying that, to getting their hands on one.

Rory Heap, the local community worker, had already been

talking to Billy Floyd and Steve Cossack, in particular, about how the Council worked. Billy wanted to persuade people in the Weller Streets area with a bit more political experience to get involved in this. Stephen Rice says, 'Billy Floyd kept saying to me, "Come to the meeting, come to the meeting."' Stephen did, but at first remained as sceptical as Peter Tyrrell and Philip Hughes, who both had some union experience behind them.

Two other young men Billy had managed to get involved were Pat Russell and Ann Byrne's husband Kevin. Pretty soon Kevin, talking it over in Wilkie's pub, came to feel something of the enthusiasm Billy and Steve had. 'I went along about the same time as Floydie. I liked the idea of setting up a co-op. I thought it was a bit of a fight and I wanted to get involved in it. When I did sort of join in it, I remember saying, "This is going to work y'know." And Billy was fucking determined. Billy was getting vibes from me and I was getting vibes from him. And there was a few people coming along – doubting Thomases.'

To the doubting Thomases the committee members laid themselves on the line. Eifion says, 'We had to keep pushing. There were a lot of people saying "You'll never do it." As a committee member I had to say to them, "We will do it."'

But how? The obvious way to get at the Council seemed to be to go through the local councillors. The ward was a solid Labour ward. Labour was the leading party on the Council, though it didn't have an overall majority. And to the likes of Billy, Steve, Rory and Kevin the co-op seemed to be a socialist idea: bringing 'power and control' that unions wielded in the workplace to bear on people's housing. Indeed, as Rory says of himself, 'My own politics at the time were incredibly naive – which I think was fortunate. I can remember discussions in the pub where it was me who was arguing very fundamentalist Labour Party social-ism that they shouldn't form a co-op.'

This 'fundamentalist' Labour line argued that a co-op would be queue-jumping: that the vital issue was that all 400 families in the Weller Streets area should be getting decent rehousing in the right place, not just the seventy-six whose names were on the register when it closed at the end of September.

The co-op committee felt that was wrong. They'd given everyone in the area a chance to join the co-op. They weren't trying to jump the queue ahead of the others in the area, as they saw it: just do something for themselves. So, Steve Cossack recounts, 'We went round all the local councillors saying, "This is who we are." They said, "In the whole of District E there's no land to give you." We had to enter on to a political campaign then; on top of which we had our own co-op learning to do.'

'District E' was the Corpie's name for the inner south end of Liverpool, stretching from the derelict docklands, through the terraced and Council housing of Liverpool 8 to the better-off residential districts of Liverpool 17, including Aigburth. The co-op said they'd found all these sites: the councillors said there were problems with all of them, and anyway the Labour Party was against the co-op in principle.

Steve Cossack remembers the crucial disappointment for him. 'The thing that really got to me: we had a meeting in our house, we were talking to councillors about it and I was very naive – because Alec [Doswell] was my uncle. Cyril Taylor committed himself, he said – it was the manner of the man, he had such a supercilious grin on his face, he said, "You'll never do it. You'll never do it" – don't get me wrong, I like the man.'

One of the local councillors was John Hamilton, also Labour leader of the Council. In early October the committee got him to come along to a general meeting. He was conciliatory, but in the end unhelpful. 'If I could help you I would, but I can't sort of thing', is one member's recollection. That enraged Peter Tyrrell, sitting on the back benches. Eifion says, 'We had Hamilton. He'd stood up and given us the spiel. [Peter] stood up and said, "He's the only politician who's never told you any lies; he hasn't told you anything at all."' Peter says it was a bit stronger than that, and led to Billy Floyd buttonholing him to join the committee the next week: 'I think I was asked to join the committee because I fucking argued. I meant it: "He's promised you fuck all."'

John Hamilton's line was that whatever Labour wanted would be outvoted by the Liberals and Tories in Council. Nevertheless he agreed to meet a delegation from the co-op to go through in detail the sites they'd identified as possibles. This happened two weeks later. Eifion: 'We went to one of the first meetings in the Municipal Buildings with John Hamilton. We had to tell Billy not to swear. Nothing happened there. He told us nothing we didn't know already. Billy kept almost saying "F-f-f-f..."'

There was a problem with every one of the sites the co-op had come up with. There were bad ground conditions; or sites were 'zoned for open space'; or were owned by the Mersey Docks and Harbour Board, and would take long-winded administrative processes to get hold of.

As for the plum sites the Council already knew about, these were a political football. Labour, with a majority on the committees, would put them forward for Council housing. The Liberals and Tories, with a majority on the full Council, would amend that to offering them to developers for houses for sale. Billy recalls: 'One meeting with John Hamilton, we pleaded with him, "Go on, just offer us a little bit of one of your big municipal sites." And he said, "No, but I'll promise you my support for a piece of one of the municipal sites if we get them." And we said, "You know that's going to be defeated, don't you?" And he said, "Yes." So there we were.'

In this position of apparent stalemate the committee – and in particular Billy, Steve, Kevin, whoever else might be in Wilkie's at the time – turned increasingly to Rory for advice. They knew they had to be more sophisticated in their tactics when people like John Hamilton, with senior Council officers to advise him, were pouring cold water on their hopes. Rory says: 'We had meetings with senior planners where the Weller

Streets had to justify the search-for-land...That was when we began the rehearsals for meetings. We'd meet the day before and play roles. People were allocated a specific job, like Kevin or Billy would mark a particular man and stick to them.'

Yet at this time Rory himself came under pressure from his employers, the Toxteth Community Council, to reduce the time he was spending with the Weller Streets. The Community Council had been set up in the 1960s on the initiative of local Labour MP Dick Crawshaw (now an SDP peer). But it had become a moribund self-perpetuating group of local worthies, nervous of contentious political issues. Says Eifion, 'There were these same half-dozen there all the time...Some people had been on that committee for years and years.'

The Weller Streets joined in a solution to Rory's problem: they packed the Annual General Meeting, with Steve Cossack as their candidate for Chairman. In fifteen years there'd never been a contested election. The result was inevitable. 'So I,' as Steve puts it, 'in effect became Heaps's boss.'

Billy recalls: 'I remember walking from there, with the pensioners. It was the first time they all realized they had power in their right hand – just by voting. They were all singing on the way back, "We are the Weller Streets".' Steve Cossack sums it up: 'We now refer to it as the putsch. For the first time in Weller Streets' history we showed the old motto, "Unity is strength".'

But the solidarity that was emerging among people who came to co-op meetings was still a sceptical feeling. Arthur Roberts, a committee member and faithful attender of meetings, says: 'When we first started I used to think, I always used to say to 'em, "This'll never come off. It'll fall to bits." It plodded on and plodded on. I didn't think it'd come off really...And Rory used to talk about it, I think about it being going to meetings, plodding on, plodding on.'

Rory's role with the co-op had been secured, but his advice wasn't necessarily welcomed. "You'll never do it," councillors were saying it, people in the streets were saying it. But it wasn't just 'plodding on' for everyone. Kitty says, 'When it first started it was a night out for me.' She was one of the committee members who kept faith with the idea from the beginning: 'You'd be maybe walking to the shops and people'd say, "Do you think it's going to happen?" And you'd tell people, "If we stay together we'll do it."'

Billy Floyd kept trying to motivate people. He tried to keep the meetings a mixture of information and entertainment. Philip Hughes: 'I don't know if Billy knew about those T-shirts he used to wear... This zipper on his sweater come down and there'd be some rude advertisement on his chest. "Nice one, squirrel" with a picture of two squirrels...and "W/anchor". And "Your friendly neighbourhood pervert".'

Outside the meetings he kept reassuring people. Kitty says of the reason the co-op kept going at this time: 'I think it was Billy getting at them, 'cause he was the milkman then. I think he was telling 'em quite a few little white lies. And also the people knew, they knew they weren't going to get rehoused by the Corpie where they wanted to go.'

The fundamental cause of the co-op's being founded – people's housing conditions and lack of choice – still remained. Billy, Kitty and the others saw it as their job to keep faith in the idea going. Lily Faulkner: 'We had meetings and meetings and meetings. And they'd kid us up they'd got this land, and that land. It was to keep us together.'

The committee decided on a new approach to try and get the land. Approaches to Labour councillors had come to a dead end. It was from this point, in early November 1977, that the co-op became 'apolitical as far as parties were concerned, but very political as far as local politics are concerned', as Rory describes it. Partly this, anyway, was an acknowledgement of the range of political views within the co-op. But for those with any experience of politics it was done with considerable reluctance. Stephen Rice's account of his background sums this up:

'In union politics, I'd attend all the meetings and make my voice heard. At the time we were trying to oust the branch Secretary; we got him out in the end on a technicality...Then I worked behind the bar in the Labour Club on Warwick Street. I was no better and no worse than anyone who was in the place...Basically what we had to do was alienate ourselves from the Labour Party who should have been the ones helping us: 'cause they wanted this Mother Cow of municipal housing which should have gone out forty or fifty years ago.'

No one else in the co-op feels quite as strongly as that. If people could have got the kind of Corpie rehousing they wanted the co-op might never have been formed. But certainly it was ironic that, as Rory puts it: 'At the time all the three local wards were Labour-controlled. Our battles were with the Labour establishment, not with the Liberals.' (It must however be borne in mind that this view reflects Rory's own battles with the Community Council, as well as the co-op's own mainstream affairs.)

So the co-op broadened its line of attack. They put together all the information they'd gathered about sites in District E, and put a strong covering letter to it. Billy, Kevin and Rory put it together in Rory's office. Rory: 'I remember I just sat down at the typewriter and we did the thing.' It became known as the 'Bomb'. It went to every Liverpool city councillor and to officials in the planning and housing departments.

The committee also made deliberate efforts to cultivate councillors of other parties. After housing committee meetings they got hold of Mervyn Kingston, the Tory spokesman on housing, and Trevor Jones, the leader of the Liberals. Billy Floyd remembers going to committee meetings: 'We were getting minutes of the sub-committees and we knew more of what they [the councillors] were doing than they did...We knew where all the technical officers sat in sub-committee meetings. The tea ladies used to give us the tea first. Ken

54

Stewart [Labour chairman] used to say there was nothing on the agenda for us today. We'd say, we'd just like to sit here and see how it's done.'

In amongst these negotiations and lobbying, Rory says, 'There was a very delicate period. Because there was an obvious site: Jolliffe Street. They were talking about rehousing the whole area: 400 units.' Jolliffe Street was a site soon to be cleared, half a mile to the north of the Weller Streets, towards Princes Avenue. The other side of Princes Avenue is Granby: a high proportion of Liverpool's black population lives there. Princes Avenue itself has a reputation for 'vice', because of the clubs along it, and for muggings, among people from the Park Road end of Liverpool 8. Kitty says, 'We were thinking of our kids coming home on the bus and getting picked up on the way home from school...Not one said, "Yes, we want to live on the Jolliffe Street site."' In any event, the 'they' who were talking about it were Labour councillors: lacking an overall majority, they'd never get it agreed for municipal housing through the Council.*

The Liberals had another proposal up their sleeves: Hesketh Street, a site about a mile and a half from the Weller Streets towards Aigburth, in an area that during the 1970s was becoming 'gentrified'. Rory Heap summarizes the state of the parties at the crucial housing committee meeting in November 1977:

'There was the Labour Party taking a principled stand that co-ops were queue-jumping. And the Liberals keen to accommodate the co-op: but the co-op had already demonstrated it wasn't prepared to compromise on anybody's politics, just use them...Going into the meeting, the Tories were saying, "You're all right"; the Liberals were saying, "You've

---

*The site was eventually developed by Wimpey's as homes for sale; but when Labour took power locally in 1983 the homes were taken over for municipal housing.

got Hesketh Street"; Labour saying, "Beware your new-found friends".'

Beware your new-found friends: the Liberals and Conservatives allied to offer the co-op Hesketh Street. But it would only take about thirty houses; the co-op had seventy-six potential members. Billy Floyd recalls that 'on the Town Hall steps I said to Trevor Jones, "We think your giving us Hesketh Street is an effort to split the co-op. Where's the proper site?" Trevor Jones said, "We're going to get you other sites, this is just the first."'

But 'other sites' would mean people wouldn't be rehoused together; even if the promise was to be believed. The committee might, though, have said, 'OK, the first thirty'll have Hesketh Street.' Instead they proposed, not to reject the offer outright but to take a more cunning line: 'Thanks very much, but where's the real site?' Philip Hughes recalls: 'It came back to the Zion and the Council had said, "You can have Hesketh Street but there's only room for thirty houses." When I'd seen that, when they said no, I saw they were committed enough. And also they said, "We're sixty* people, we're all sticking together."'

Philip had joined the co-op with Stephen Rice. 'I remember Stephen Rice saying to me, "Are you going to throw your oar in?" And I said, "Yes, I think it's a goer, yes."' The rejection – that wasn't quite a rejection – of Hesketh Street was a turning-point in their commitment to the co-op. As it was for Peter Tyrrell: 'That was also the point where I became committed to it... I became convinced that it wasn't going to be a talking shop.'

Peter recognized, besides Billy, Steve and Kevin, the commitment others had already shown: 'They were pretty determined people: Dono, Odger, Pat Russell... Kitty and

---

*People's memories of the members involved at different stages are vague. There were still seventy-six names on the register at this stage.

Irene...I thought, even if this crowd failed they were determined to see it through; even if they failed they were going to give *them* a run for their money.' And like Billy, Kevin and Steve before him, he says his motivation was 'mainly the fight, mainly the idea: Let's take *them* on, let's see who *they* are. 'Cause your life had been fucking dominated by people you never knew. So I thought, that's for me, let's have a go at *them*.'

Philip Hughes also felt some of that 'kamikaze attitude' Stephen Rice said that the inaction of the Council had fostered. 'There'd been loads of failures in action groups. And no failures in new-build housing co-operatives because there hadn't been any. So there was nothing to lose. That's the way I saw it.'

These were the reactions of union-minded men; the Hesketh Street decision turned them decisively into supporters. For other members it was more vaguely impressive: Arthur Roberts: 'I used to be made up when they came back and told us what they'd done – that *they'd* listen to *us*. That's what they done in the early days: made everyone stand up and listen.'

At public meetings – now usually called 'general meetings', i.e. meetings of the general membership – the reports on the lobbying were still squeezed between reports on fund-raising and sessions by CDS workers on what a co-op was. 'The more I went, the more interesting it got,' says Billy Lybert, who'd originally thought it 'rubbish': but people like him were only going to be really convinced by the offer of a site big enough for the whole co-op.

Billy and Kevin got together one day with Rory Heap and Paul Lusk, who'd recently joined CDS as a co-operative education worker. Together they drafted out a leaflet, *Still No Site for the Weller Streets Co-op*. A small group of committee members lobbied councillors as they went into the Council meeting of 14 December, and handed them copies of the leaflet (overleaf).

A message for councillors attending the Liverpool City Council meeting, 14th December 1977.

Still No Site for Weller Streets Co-op

We are eighty families in a clearance area off Park Road. We have been active as a group for over a year, and are now registered as a Friendly Society. We have appointed our Development Agents, and will soon be registered with the Housing Corporation as a housing association. We need 5 acres in District E for an 80 unit new-build development.

Following detailed discussions with Council members and officials, the Weller Streets Co-op in mid-November provided all councillors, departments and other interested bodies with a report containing details of our history, a breakdown of nine potential sites and an urgent request for action.

On 14th November a special meeting of the Housing Committee considered a report of the Director of Housing (DH 446/7/77) concerning rehousing in advance of CPO and municipal housebuilding projections.

On Agenda Item 2, the Committee resolves that: "...the Stage 1A clearance lands at Hesketh Street be developed with housing for rent by a Housing Co-operative, provided that the families to be rehoused are drawn from the Weller Streets clearance area in the light of the recent establishment of the Weller Streets Housing Co-operative." Councillors will note that this is **NOT** a proposal to offer a site to the Weller Streets Co-op; it is a proposal to offer rehousing to **SOME** of our members on a site which can in fact hold only 30 units. It is, therefore, a proposal to break up the Weller Streets Co-operative.

On Agenda Item 3, the Committee asked for a report from the City Planning Officer, on whether additional land in the South City area could be used to assist in the fulfilment of the City's housing renewal programme. This report (CPO 441/77) was to be presented to the Housing Committee on 24th November.

But on 24th November, under Agenda Item A21 (reports DH446 and CPO 441/77), the Committee resolved (minute 292a) that: "All sites detailed in report DH446/77 . . . be included in the municipal housebuilding programme, with development of housing for rent." This report does not include the sites detailed in CPO 441/77, which contains many sites identified by the Weller Streets Co-op.

CPO 441/77 was not discussed and, despite the presentation of material on available sites by both the City Planning Officer and the Weller Streets Housing Co-op, no further progress has been made by the City in providing us with a suitable site for our 80 units.

We appeal to ALL Councillors IRRESPECTIVE of party loyalties to consider the following facts:

- We still have no land, and until we have land, we cannot begin to use the Government funds available for co-operative schemes.
- We can all see that there is plenty of idle land in District E for which no viable use can be foreseen.
- Much of this land could be used for rental housing if it were re-zoned.
- Without substantial new building of housing on re-zoned sites, there is no foreseeable end to the clearance crisis.

We appeal to all Parties to use Weller Streets as a test-case for new-build co-ops on Merseyside. All we need is your permission to build on 5 acres in District E.

Our members are available and ready to answer any questions that may arise at this meeting.

Help Us to House Ourselves

Published by the Weller Streets Housing Co-operative Limited. Chairman, Billy Floyd, 62 Pecksniff Street, Liverpool 8.

The Council meeting itself was a disappointment. The offer of Hesketh Street remained; attitudes didn't seem to have shifted. Paul Lusk's first encounter with Labour councillors echoed the co-op's: 'I remember Cyril Taylor saying to me, "CDS should come down on the Weller Streets like a ton of bricks." They saw it as wrecking the strategy, jumping the queue.'

But, Billy Odger recalls, 'Me and Georgie Millington got that Ken Stewart inside. He said, "I'll fix up a meeting."' Ken Stewart, chairman of the housing committee, wrote a week later to say the meeting was fixed for 25 January; he'd get representatives of all parties together to discuss the Weller Streets' search for a site.

By the time that meeting came around, though, there'd been unexpected developments on the land issue. The co-op had known all along that the Council owned most of a site at the corner of Miles Street and Byles Street (known as 'Miles/Byles'), less than a half a mile from the Weller Streets area along Park Road. The site would take around sixty units, and was one of a number referred by the Council to housing associations early in 1977. The co-op knew CDS wanted it for their own tenants in clearance areas.

But a lot of CDS's 'clearance tenants' were in the Weller Streets Co-op. Maybe Hesketh Street would be big enough for CDS's needs; Miles/Byles might be big enough for the co-op.

There was a snag, though. A road-line went through the middle of the site, with such an effect on the development potential that when Catherine Meredith, Director of CDS, raised it with someone in another housing association, he 'pissed himself laughing at the idea we were going to develop it'. Catherine now set about trying to sort out the problem: 'What became clear was, the city was against the road, and didn't see any purpose to it. But the county still had it.'

The county council were responsible for roads; the city

council for planning permission. The city would have to consult the county about the road. So, Catherine says, 'What we decided to do was put in a planning application. The city didn't answer within the statutory period. We put in the first appeal forms. You see, it was the final leg of something; it didn't connect with anything.'

The road-line was an ambitious scheme to widen and divert Park Road which seemed unlikely ever to happen. So Catherine had set the wheels in motion. She also saw that one key problem for the co-op might be 'nominations'. Even if the co-op could get its site, it might, as the price for having public money invested in the scheme, have to offer 50 per cent of lettings to tenants nominated by the Council.

Catherine had formerly worked in the housing department. Just before Christmas she invited herself into the housing manager's office for a drop of festive cheer. She came out having convinced him of the logic that there should be no council nominations on the Weller Streets scheme, on the grounds that the co-op would be housing people the Council would otherwise have a duty to rehouse.

All this – the dealings on the road-line, and on nominations – was done without the co-op's knowledge. Catherine Meredith, for CDS, didn't want to raise the co-op's hopes when it all might fall through; 'putting on a front' as the committee did to its own members. But Paul Lusk, new on the scene and enthused by the idea of the co-op, took it into his hands: 'I was seeing Weller that night and [Catherine] told me not to tell the co-op the swap was on and I'd decided to tell them. I did it because I wanted Weller to move as fast as possible and I didn't want the committee to get snarled up in looking for a site – the irrational motive being, wanting the glory.'

That caused ructions. A deputation from the Weller Streets 'invaded the management committee' of CDS in January, Paul recalls, and made their views clear. The next day Paul got a dressing down. 'In retrospect I would have done the same thing again. Had that been allowed to drift things could have turned out very differently.'

So by the time the meeting Ken Stewart had agreed to came around, at the end of January 1978, the co-op and CDS were ready to propose jointly a swap of Hesketh Street for Miles/ Byles. Adrian Moran was one of the CDS contingent: 'They were on that side of the table, we were on this, the officers were scattered about. The key thing we wanted to get over as CDS was to establish the credibility of Weller Streets in terms of their organization as a housing association, and as far as possible the Housing Corporation would fund in principle so the site wouldn't lay vacant... It was a big meeting for what appeared to be a fairly minor issue. I came away with the impression that it was done: none of the parties objected.'

It's a reflection of the co-op's political success that their 'minor issue' attracted a 'big meeting' of all three parties. So the swap was on provided the road-line could be moved. Catherine Meredith got some help from Margaret Simey, the local county councillor, whom she knew, and whom the co-op valued, as Kate Kelly says: 'The only councillor that really had faith in us was Margaret Simey... She knew that they'd get away. I think, when she saw how determined they were, she wanted them to do it.'

Catherine got a meeting with Kenneth Thompson, then Chairman of the County Council. 'He called in the engineer. Our case was, they could ease the road without taking that full land take. They removed their objection two days before it would have gone to [planning] appeal.'

So the site could now be developed. The informal agreement in January with leaders of the three parties took a while to get through the cycle of Council committee meetings. So it wasn't until 19 April, eight months after the first meeting of the co-op, that the Council formally resolved to offer the Miles/Byles site to the Weller Streets Co-op.

Committee members celebrated in Wilkie's. Stephen Rice says: 'I don't think the Weller Streets was a real force until the site got allocated. From that point on it was all systems go.'

It was for the committee. It affirmed their standing to the outside world. Yet it had little effect on the rest of the membership. 'They gave us promises, the committee gave us promises,' Billy Lybert says. This was the latest in a long line of 'promises': most people would believe it when it was signed sealed and delivered.

So the co-op's development continued gradually, regardless of the apparent importance of events like the offer of Miles/ Byles. Some of the more cautious members were getting more involved. Sammy Roberts, for instance, the former moderate shop steward on the docks, had been under pressure from his son Arthur, and from Billy Floyd. As he summarizes his conversion to the idea: 'They came around, Billy Floyd and a few more. They had a little committee trying to form this co-op. He kept harping on me. I thought about it for a while. I thought, it's better joining than not. The consequences was, I thought, there's something going on here. I started going round myself then, getting other people to join in.'

Sammy and another retired docker, Dickie Sharp, came on to the committee. But there were still sceptics. Kate Kelly used to say to her daughter Kitty, '"D'you really think it'll come off? Youse'll be on your old age pension before you'll get out of there." She used to say to me, "Here, read that." And it was all double Dutch.'

The growing, but still small, band of people who believed in the idea, the 'fight', pressed on in the hope that the detailed negotiations over the site wouldn't have any hitches. And they kept pressing people to keep coming to general meetings. And people did keep coming, partly, as Irene Stead says, 'Cause it wasn't all serious: it was a laugh as well.' Philip Hughes, used to union and Labour Party meetings, says, 'It was slapdash in a way, but it wasn't. Billy was sorting through it. I was more into disciplined meetings. It would have been a lot more boring. He was getting things done and it was a laugh. To keep people entertained Billy was the prime catalyst: getting everybody to do what he wanted them to do.' And in eight months the co-op had moved a long way from being a 'crazy idea'. Now it was a force to be reckoned with; an organization with a growing number of committed members and with a site, and money to build on it, available in principle; an organization that hung on to its roots and its sense of humour as it moved on to new challenges.

3

On Tap, Not on Top:
Elites and Professionals

The co-op's story proper continues with the design of the estate in Chapter 4. But it seems worthwhile to step back at this point – as some of the co-op did, in March and April 1978 – and review how far they'd got and what they'd achieved.

People's memories are fickle. Often they remember what they want to remember, and impose a shape and pattern on events which wasn't really there at the time. Thus Stephen Rice describes the search for land as 'a very Billy Floyd type strategy: it worked out brilliantly . . . to aim for the sun and get the moon. It became a lot easier, from the bargaining point of view, to forgo Aigburth and get a brick field in the Dingle.'

Many committee members describe the search for land in similar terms, as a deliberate strategy to get what they wanted, to 'ask for the prime sites and they'll palm us off with something' as Alec Caddis puts it. Billy Floyd himself is inclined to reply, 'Yes, that was the strategy – as it developed.' It didn't start off that way. One thing led to another: from the crazy idea to the complicated business; from taxi trips looking at sites to hob-nobbing with the leaders of Liverpool's political parties; from aiming for Aigburth because that was what people really wanted, to aiming for Aigburth in order to get 'a brick field in the Dingle'. Rory Heap describes the committee's approach as a 'kind of bridgehead mentality: we've got this far, we've got to take the next step. They never understood the problem as a whole. They only ever saw it in stages.'

So when Rory himself describes the review that took place in March/April, the same reservations need to be borne in mind: that at the time the review took place, it was trying to find a pattern in what had already happened; and that his memory is recorded five years after the event. Here's how he describes it:

'At the point where the land deal was clinched there was a bit of a reassessment. There was lots of big talk in CDS. I remember we sat down and tried to discuss what people had learnt:

(1) politicians are to be used and abused;
(2) to set up a project of that nature you need professional support;
(3) you don't trust it.'

The 'we' who sat down to discuss it, the 'people' who'd done this learning weren't the whole co-op, nor even the management committee in full, but the group of young men who'd got to know one another through the co-op and who'd talk about things over a pint in Wilkie's: Billy, Kevin, Steve, Rory, and lately Philip Hughes and Peter Tyrrell. The discussion itself probably took place in Wilkie's: one of those pubs still standing when the buildings it used to be attached to have been demolished; when the clientele it used to serve have moved on. It's dark, little frequented. There's a sense of deals being struck in quiet corners.

Some of what Rory says has the macho bravado the atmosphere of the pub helps to generate. 'Politicians are to be used and abused' is one over-statement that comes from that. In practice the intensive lobbying of councillors and officials had meant that when the luck needed to fall the co-op's way – over the site swap – they were in a position to exploit it. And what they'd achieved in the political arena was a big move forwards from the action group days when 'they' kept the women on the pavement and graciously allowed Ann Caddis five minutes to speak. The co-op had taken 'them' on and won one victory.

The question of 'professionals' is more complicated. The word 'professional' itself means a lot of different things to different people. To architects, solicitors, administrators it means a qualified worker in certain kinds of white-collar job: they wouldn't regard CDS workers as 'professionals'. They'd also apply it to a certain standard of work, a 'professional' job. Billy Floyd uses it in this sense, talking in the early days about the committee trying to look 'professional to our own people', meaning competent, efficient, polished – with overtones of not necessarily telling the whole truth.

But to people in the Weller Streets 'professional' had more to do with class. Professionals were the people who left their cosy offices at five o'clock and drove down Park Road looking straight ahead, on their way to the comfortable suburbs, leaving people in the Weller Streets in their slums.

Rory had a foot in both camps. When talking about not trusting professional support, he clearly doesn't see himself as a 'professional'. But he was a community worker, paid to work with local people. Ann Caddis and a few others had already known him before the co-op got started: 'He'd come to us and say, "They're taking off the Number 3 bus, can you help us with a petition about it?" And they still took off the Number 3 bus but it was a mutual – whenever you wanted Rory for a bit of advice, you'd get it.'

Ann had been used to dealing with Rory's predecessor as community worker; she accepted him and his role readily. But Rory himself had felt unsure of his standing locally before the co-op began: 'I had no local credibility at all except through Steve Cossack who I'd only talked to in the boozer a few times. I think he just walked in once and said, "What are you going to do about this housing action?"'

So Rory came along to the action group meeting that was to decide whether to try and form a co-op. What Steve Cossack had recalled as 'a spontaneous reaction from the floor' at that meeting is remembered differently by Billy Floyd: 'There was utter fucking chaos. And this voice was coming through: "Don't make any decisions now – why don't you have a working party?" Everyone else was shouting across one another. I wanted to know who this guy was with the fucking articulate voice that spread so much calm.'

It was Rory. From that intervention at the public meeting, he worked closely with the co-op throughout its formative period. When the 'Bomb' was being prepared, he says, 'I remember I just sat down at the typewriter and we did the thing. That formed the basis of how we worked. So, anything that was done, was done by the co-op. I was just working with them.' Later, when he was an adviser on tactics for important meetings, 'My role in that was like a tutor on a course. I made sure they themselves knew what they were doing, but I wasn't interested in what they were doing. I was just a human tape recorder.'

Billy says the advisory role was Rory's central task with the co-op: 'Alongside all this, Rory was working with five or six of us on the politics of the whole thing.'

But it wasn't just a question of 'roles', of Rory being 'uninterested' in what they were doing. He became bound up with the whole idea himself. It gave his own work a new meaning. He didn't do anything else, he says, for a year and a half as a community worker. A personal loyalty built up on both sides. Co-op members tend to play it down, but Sue Jackson of CDS thinks his blindness played a part in this: 'Because he was blind, they could offer him a lot of support which none of the other people involved with them needed. Rory was absolutely vital for them sticking at it – when there was nothing else, nothing on paper, just a dream.'

'People were high on an idea,' Rory says. 'Other people didn't know what the fuck was going on. There was a third group knew what was going on, but didn't know where it'd lead.' Rory himself was part of the group that was 'high on an idea', the idea of a fight, a mission, a mini-revolution, not merely a way of getting decent housing for themselves. It was a strain too: 'I had a very bad time working for you lot. I was more worried about being acceptable to you lot than to the Community Council. Not to the whole co-op, of course, 'cause it wasn't that kind of deal; but to the core activists.'

Rory worked for the 'core activists' of the co-op, not for the people who paid his wages. When his formal employers cut up rough about that, the co-op took over his employers. They'd cut through the paraphernalia of accountability and made Rory one of their own. And he, in turn, had helped to shape their development.

The other 'professional' who worked closely with the co-op in the early days was Sue Jackson of CDS. With her there was no question of wooing her away from her employers: CDS, although a young organization, already had twenty or so staff working at its Liverpool 8 office in Geraint Street and its head office in town.

But, as with Rory, a strong personal relationship built up between Sue and members of the co-op. They felt they'd struck a personal deal with her, according to Alec Caddis: 'Sue Jackson was fighting with us. She asked, could she work for us? And we said, if we can get people interested, yes.' Billy Floyd: 'Sue saw it as part of her work commitment but it was in her own time. She was operating as a sort of Lone Ranger.'

Two people Sue became particularly friendly with were Kitty Heague and her mother Kate Kelly. Kate says, 'We couldn't have done without them [CDS] – especially Sue Jackson. She was great, she'd come and sit amongst you. Any co-op needs someone like that at the beginning.'

Sue didn't particularly put herself across as representing CDS in her work with the Weller Streets. So people talk about her 'working at risk' or of 'robbing' paperwork out of CDS when, as she recalls it, it was all part of the job. As Irene Stead saw the distinction between Sue and CDS: 'I think Sue Jackson got a lot done for us. We didn't have a lot to do with CDS in those days. It was Sue Jackson and she was great.'

CDS as an organization wasn't considered 'great'. For a start it had years of distrust of 'landlords' to overcome. Rory's suspicions of them, apparent in his remarks about 'big talk' once the land deal was secured, were shared by the leading members of the committee. As Stephen Rice – himself critical of Rory for being a 'hard liner' on politics – saw the distinction, Rory 'was very working-class and he could relate a lot easier with the plight than the comfortable middle-class CDS people'. So, at that time 'he was much cleverer and much more professional than anybody at CDS, in a cunning sort of way.'

Stephen, like the other 'core activists', was in his late twenties, newly married, born and brought up in the streets off Park Road. He'd been modestly active in union and Labour politics. But he was different from the others in important ways. He'd been to Quarry Bank School in Allerton rather than a local secondary. He'd felt out of place with the suburban kids there; but the experience had left him more conventionally ambitious than the other young men. His wife wasn't from the area, and wanted them to buy a house in the suburbs; but he was interested in the co-op idea, and wanted to get involved.

Later he was to be criticized within the co-op for allying himself too closely with CDS. But initially he was as wary as anybody. 'I saw them as a gang of middle-class student types and I'm suspicious of student types inasmuch as they're all trendy left-wingers. It took them six months to say who they were, what they were. Now, nobody had ever given us anything in our lives. It took me a bit of time to come to terms with the fact that they were pretty genuine.'

Arthur Roberts, on the committee from the first, says of CDS: 'At first they were the brains and we were the mugs. You'd get told: "They're not getting paid for it, they believe in it."' The ideas of 'giving us something', of 'believing in it' were important from the beginning.

Co-op members were dubious of people just working with them for the money: such people would have more in common with the 'them' the fight was against, than with the 'us' of the co-op. And there was a strong contrast between Sue Jackson and the other people they met from CDS at this time. A few of them had met Catherine Meredith, the director, in the Bold Street office in town. She seemed a remote figure, a bit of a bureaucrat, speaking softly so you had to strain to hear, her expression hidden behind darkened glasses.

Adrian Moran was another who wouldn't – as Sue Jackson would – 'come and sit amongst you'. His active support for the co-op behind the scenes, for example in arguing its case with public bodies, was unknown to co-op members. Instead they saw him standing at the front in co-op meetings, trying to explain about co-ops and housing associations and the rules and regulations. 'Adrian Moran used to come to educate us but he never – it was just lines on a blackboard,' says Irene. Philip Hughes recalls: 'He came in and said, "You're going to borrow a million pounds"....We all used to go upstairs and have bits of paper and get it explained, how we were going to get a million pounds.'

Harry Dono sums up what it was like to be a committee member, seeing this education programme at work: 'You've got to break it down into language they can understand. You can't throw the dictionary at them. Sue Jackson – she could break it down and make you understand. Adrian Moran – he started talking over and above what they can understand. They might agree with you there and then but by the time they've got home they're coming knocking at your door saying, "What does this mean?"'

Sue's relaxed style and Rory's brand of education 'like a tutor on a course' were more acceptable than echoes of the schoolroom. But Sue and Rory both worked mostly with a small, committed group of committee members. Adrian's brief was broader, trying to cover more ground with more people. He says, 'The whole thing is complex. You've got to get across complex concepts: the bureaucratic hoops and hurdles.'

It was a necessary stage to go through, even if people didn't like the style. And the committee wanted CDS people to give talks at general meetings, because, as Stephen Rice recalls, 'I said early on, if we're not careful we're going to be an elitist group here, an us and them situation.' 'Education' was intended to try and bridge the gulf between committee members, learning fast, and the rest of the membership lagging behind. So, Adrian Moran says, 'When we did presentations to general meetings the purpose in part was to explain what the committee was doing – demystifying it for the ordinary member so they didn't feel left out.' The other part of the purpose was to keep people interested when there wasn't much to report. Billy Floyd says it was like buttering a piece of bread; they didn't have much butter and they spread it very thinly.

As things turned out, the main CDS workers with the co-op weren't to be Sue and Adrian, but Paul Lusk and Martine Gouilleux. Paul joined CDS in November 1977 specially to work with co-ops, and immediately plunged into working with the Weller Streets. 'I probably elbowed Sue out of the way,' he says. 'I just wanted to get in on the action.'

Paul had done teaching and a bit of journalism before. He didn't know much about Liverpool or about co-ops, so when he first got the job, 'My image of what I'd do was going round houses in these improvement areas working with the children 'cause they'd be the co-ops of the future. Once I'd met Weller I became very clear that the idea had much more potential. And that it was like working [abroad]: learning a different language, with people with different perceptions: an outsider myself.'

Straight away he got involved in writing the *Still No Site for the Weller Streets Co-op* leaflet. 'That was done at a meeting of Billy, Kevin Byrne, Rory Heap and me. Billy and Kevin, their style was a kind of ministerial style: we're here to make the decisions: you brief us.'

From then on Paul took on most of the 'educational' work with the co-op. His style didn't go down any better than Adrian's had. Peter Tyrrell remembers: 'One early comment that used to piss me off was, "You're a group of ordinary people." I mean, what are extraordinary people like? People with two fucking heads?' Paul's diagrams became a bit of a standing joke in the co-op. 'We asked him one night, "Where's Custer? There's enough arrows on that board for him."'

Slide projectors wouldn't work, films would start to be shown upside down. People were both annoyed and amused. It was clear that Paul was learning along with the co-op, and maybe it was handy sometimes to have him there as the butt of Billy's or Kevin's or Philip's humour. Paul remembers the state of ignorance he was working from: 'None of us knew anything. None of us knew about new-build. We were sitting there desperately trying to find books about new-build.' He accepts the early talks were a failure: 'I remember very solemnly declaiming from the front. I wasn't in any fit state mentally or by experience to mount an education programme.'

As far as CDS went, 'We were useful to them politically but that was it. The education came later really.' But Paul himself got drawn in personally. He and his girlfriend would pop round to the Floyds' house in Pecksniff Street and end up sharing a bottle of whisky and dinner. He'd be a bit indiscreet sometimes about what was happening in CDS, especially in Wilkie's. 'I suppose the very heavy drinking is part of it. When you got involved with them you got involved with their generosity and . . . this atmosphere of menace. It's very exciting to share with people of more or less my own age this political vision. It reflected the political ideals I'd formed at seventeen or eighteen but never actually done anything about.'

With the 'atmosphere of menace' in Wilkie's went a sense of conspiracy among the leading co-op members: that if anyone really understood how radically different the co-op was, they'd squash it. This drew Paul in: in CDS itself he was regarded as an oddball, opposed to the 'welfare housing management' he encountered there: early on he found his allies among the Weller Streets.

By April 1978 Paul, along with the 'core activists', recognized that the day-to-day business of the co-op was getting more complicated. Different people had begun to specialize in different things, largely on Billy's initiative. He'd say, 'Why don't you have a go at so-and-so?' And mostly people did.

So Kevin, with his experience in the building trade, was going to specialize in design along with Alec Caddis and Harry Dono; Kitty, Irene, Ann Byrne and Thelma Floyd worked on fund-raising ideas; Stephen Rice was interested in the education side of things: 'I was nominated for the information/ education role, which I was glad to take on 'cause it was certainly the most creative part of the whole thing. I wasn't interested in bricks and mortar. I was interested in putting the ideas across.'

Paul suggested the specialization could be formalized by having a number of sub-committees. The management committee went along with the idea. The management committee members were to go on each sub-committee: two design groups, membership, development agreement with CDS, information/education, and fund-raising. It was hoped that more ordinary members would be drawn in by the ideas of working in small groups. In practice that didn't happen. Most of the people who were prepared to put time into the co-op were already on the committee, or doing fund-raising work. And to the ordinary member it probably looked a pretty heavy job now, to be a committee member, to understand what was going on.

Alongside all this, and in addition to the 'education' work, CDS from early on did most of the administrative work involved in setting up the co-op. The co-op dealt with attendance and membership registers, the issue of shares from March 1978, and did their own minutes. CDS dealt with the powers-that-be. In December 1977 the co-op's registration as an 'industrial and provident society' had come through. CDS then helped them to apply for registration with the Housing Corporation, the government body the money – hopefully – was coming from. And when the Miles/Byles site was secured in principle, CDS handled all the paperwork related to that. Much of this – the letters, phone calls, files – was then and remained invisible to the co-op; a few of them came to appreciate the extent of it later on.

Martine Gouilleux* had gradually taken over responsibility for this administrative work in CDS. She was a desk woman, at home with meticulous files and correspondence. The Weller Streets didn't know what to make of this Frenchwoman in her twenties. Sue Jackson says that at first, 'I know that Martine felt there was quite a lot of suspicion about her, particularly among the women, 'cause the women weren't used to dealing with someone like Martine, who looked quite flirtatious, but wasn't.'

Once the sub-committees were formed she joined in with a questionnaire group interviewing members about their home situation. She only lived half a mile away; they had one or two meetings in her flat; another personal commitment cautiously began.

Yet however committed the individuals were, the people at CDS were still seen as fundamentally different from the Weller Streets people. Arthur Roberts sums this up, comparing CDS workers with Rory Heap: 'They used to throw things at us. He'd ask them questions so they'd have to answer us in our own way without the...bureaucracy. Maybe they didn't know how to do it any better until Rory who knew both sides could

---

* Martine has since returned to France and hasn't contributed to the writing of this story.

explain it to them...I think he was great: he's in their field but he's on our side.'

And there had to be something more than personal deals struck between the co-op and the individual professionals who worked with them. A contract, a 'development agreement' was needed between the co-op and CDS. The sub-committee dealing with this discussed CDS's proposals with the co-op's recently-appointed solicitor, John Ashby. Usually the sub-committees met in CDS's Geraint Street office, but that didn't seem right for this situation. So, as Philip Hughes recalls: 'We used to meet in the back room at Wilkie's. When we first got this agreement from CDS, by going through it we found all sorts of [things we disagreed with]. We'd made a list of what we thought was wrong with it. There was no disputes procedure, there was no appeals, and they still wanted something out of it in the end...'

The 'something out of it' was money. At first negotiations were handled by Adrian Moran for CDS. He was conscious of setting a precedent for other co-ops that might follow; he felt that CDS would make a loss on the work. Passions were inflamed by a letter in which he suggested that if the co-op were to pay CDS the real cost of the administrative work, 'the Weller Streets would have to spend all of their time fund-raising.' Paul says of the negotiations: 'Adrian had to do it by himself. What he did was, in the same session tell them what CDS would do and how much money they'd pay us...You could see Phil Hughes gradually realizing it was their money.'

'Their money' was the several thousand pounds' worth of administrative allowances the co-op would receive if the scheme went ahead. Money was a sensitive subject. The co-op suspected people who only worked for its sake with them. The idea of 'borrowing a million pounds' had seemed like a joke to them: this was their first encounter with the reality of it. And now CDS wanted 90 per cent of the co-op's allowances; *and* for the co-op to pay any VAT that might be payable, even though this couldn't be recouped from the government.

The co-op's representatives weren't happy with this. And within CDS the tensions between the workers exploded. The Weller Streets got drawn in. Stephen Rice got drawn in too. He was working closely with Paul by this time on education and newsletters, but he didn't like what was going on. 'Then I noticed', he says, 'there was this big power battle within CDS, with the people that came down to the meetings...They also tried to use us, the Weller Streets, as pawns in the game. Straight away I told Floydie not to get involved. It worried me. I thought, if that's the kind of professionalism we're involved with, then God help us.'

The co-op committee were bewildered, but did get involved. The outcome was that Adrian Moran got taken off the Weller Streets work; and that the committee got some insight into the kind of back-stabbing these 'professionals', for all their enthusiasm for the Weller Streets, sometimes got up to.

So the final negotiations over money were done with the boss, Catherine Meredith, with whom committee members felt no great rapport. The Weller Streets prepared themselves thoroughly, as they'd learnt through working with Rory. Some of the men talked it over in Wilkie's; and at the management committee 'it was agreed that the sub-committee stance at the meeting should not be threatening to CDS, but should take a hard bargaining position in the hope of getting a fair alliance for both sides which is based upon open discussion of financial requirements.'

But at the crunch meeting in CDS's offices, in August 1978, it was CDS that held to a 'hard bargaining position'. Privately Catherine might be just as excited as her staff about the Weller Streets: 'Then we didn't understand any more than they did the scale of what we were getting into. But we all believed we could make the impossible possible.'

Nevertheless, she also had a business to run. 'I did think they felt they'd got us over a barrel,' she recalls. 'They felt we should drop the percentage that they paid us. We couldn't

afford to do that. It's around the time the Co-operative
Housing Agency was falling apart,* co-operative housing had
no future; we'd spent vast amounts of time on the Weller
Streets and expected to go on doing so. They asked us to prove
what we'd spent so far.'

She'd got Martine to analyse staff time spent on the Weller
Streets. The figures showed what Adrian had maintained, that
CDS would make a loss on its work with the co-op. 'If they
hadn't asked the exercise would never have been done; but it
happened in a climate when they believed we were making a
mint out of them.' She agreed CDS would pay any VAT, and
would provide a four-stage financial statement of what they
spent on the Weller Streets work. Apart from that she
wouldn't budge.

The minutes of the next management committee are self-
explanatory: 'CDS came across as a benevolent society who by
their goodwill were allowing the Weller Streets 10 per cent of
the management percentage. It was recognized that the
committee had learnt an important lesson, particularly in
terms of being prepared and well informed...'

To the co-op's general membership this, and much of the
detail of the Weller Streets' dealings with CDS and other
professionals, was all rather vague. But the general impression
stuck: that CDS was an odd mixture of business and idealism;
of people who wanted to put something into the co-op and
people who wanted to use it; of professional front and behind-
the-scenes backbiting.

It was all much more complicated than their other dealings
with professionals. By this time Rob Macdonald, an
architectural student, was doing the co-op's minutes in

*The Co-operative Housing Agency was a quasi-separate part of the Housing
Corporation, set up under the Labour government to stimulate co-ops. It was
because of its existence that a proportion of government funds had been set
aside for housing co-ops.

exchange for help with his research for a thesis. The architect Bill Halsall had been appointed, and was coming along to evening meetings in his own time. Rory was still around. And yet here were CDS, totting up the hours they spent at co-op meetings and converting them into pound notes. The irony that 'if they hadn't asked the exercise would never have been done' only made it more bitter to swallow. Here were people who'd never quite be working for the co-op, because they'd be working for the organization called CDS too.

Their partnership continued. But there was a tension in it from then on, on both sides. Catherine Meredith says '"Professionals should be at their beck and call" – they'd got that attitude.' Seen from the co-op's point of view there's a subtle difference: 'It's like the old saying: You've got to be on tap, not on top.'

4

Now Here's the Monkey:
Designing the Scheme

By February 1978 a local firm of architects, Building Design Group (BDG) had done some sketches for CDS of what might be done on the Miles/Byles site, to help with the problems over the road-line. The committee realized they needed to start thinking about how the design might work. Billy Floyd made contact with a local architect who'd done some 'community'-type projects. After they'd met in a pub, the architect wrote recommending himself and a number of other firms – none of them local except his own.

Billy talked about it to Kevin Byrne. The two of them had become close friends through the co-op. They called themselves, and others called them, Big Bird and Little Bird: Kevin was 'Garrincha – little bird on the wing'. Billy was big and broad, Kevin slight and balding; Billy was outgoing, Kevin quieter till he got to know you; Billy was the conniver, the motivator, Kevin the one with loads of ideas, ideas he found it hard to express; Billy was the vague socialist who'd started to enjoy the 'politics' of the co-op, Kevin was the individualist who'd been in the Communist Party.

They pushed each other to stick with the co-op. Kevin remembers: 'I said to him one night, "Shall we fuck off on the ale and not go?" So we made a pact: if I don't call for you, you call for me, 'cause sometimes I didn't feel like going. We made a deal; shook hands on it. Sick or sure, we're gonna go. You'd come home from work, tired, just wanting to go to bed...'

Kevin worked as a hod-carrier, which meant that he organized the work for himself and the two brickies he worked with, and that he'd often come home tired, with an aching back. Nevertheless he kept going to the meetings. And in the back of his mind he started to think about how the houses might look, remembering all the jobs he'd been on. He drove round in his VW looking at some of them. One trip was to a new estate in Kirby, just outside Liverpool up the East Lancs. 'One of the guys I was working with, he lived up there, had told me Ribblers Lane was pretty tasty. And I had a walk across this site and it looked good. Mm, we could put pot plants there...' He took Billy up there one weekend. They both liked the feeling of the place, with houses grouped in small, secluded courtyards off quiet access roads.

Around this time one of Paul Lusk's 'education' sessions had pointed out that, to apply for Housing Corporation approval to buy the land, you needed to have an 'outline scheme' of how the houses might look. It was getting more urgent to appoint an architect. But how would they operate? Nobody had given much thought, when the co-op was formed, to what the houses might look like. 'Houses' were what everyone imagined: they lived in houses already, 'doll's houses they used to call them': they didn't want anything less. 'Flats' meant Council flats, nobody wanted that: walk-ups or high-rise or, for the elderly, 'pensioner's flats', where you couldn't live next door to your friends or relatives, and wouldn't see people passing as you did in the terraced streets.

Apart from that, and what had passed through Kevin's and Billy's minds, the idea of the design was vague. The land had to be got hold of, before it was worth thinking about what to put on it.

Among the 'professionals' too, nobody knew much. Catherine Meredith had trained as an architect but never practised; anyway, she stayed in the background as far as the co-op went. The front-line workers for CDS, and Rory Heap, had little experience of design and building. People in CDS knew what co-ops doing improvement work did: a co-op chose its own architect or surveyor, and the co-op, or its individual member/tenants, made some decisions about the way the house was improved.

In practice the choice such a co-op got didn't amount to much. Sometimes people would be able to pick where the bathroom was going to go, though if that involved adding on a back extension, it might be turned down on cost grounds by the Housing Corporation. Otherwise 'choice' boiled down to things like what colour your bathroom suite was – if you could cough up the extra cost against a white one – and how you arranged your kitchen units. Co-ops doing improvement work didn't really have any more influence over the development of their housing than tenants of the more sensitive housing associations. Costs and the structure of the house decided what you'd get.

New building was different. The Weller Streets could, if they wanted, have some influence over the way the whole estate was designed. But they'd have to work out some way of convincing an architect that that was a good idea. The subject came up at a committee meeting in late March:

> Architects are to be approached, to see if they agree with tenants participation in design of houses. Adrian reported that architects are already on site, sorting out boundaries and testing soil, etc. (nothing to do with design of units) so this will cause a bit of a hold up if we do not want them. Rory said not to indicate that we want architects to do the job definitely.

It wasn't just Rory that felt that. Billy and Kevin already had their own ideas. Why should they have to 'see if they agree' to tenant participation, when as they knew from Paul Lusk the co-op would be employing the architect? They were worried CDS were going to foist BDG off on them. Catherine Meredith came to a special committee meeting the following week to clear the air. As the minutes record:

> C. Meredith explained about local [BDG] architects and out of town, and she impressed that local are more suitable, and sympathetic, and have knowledge of New Build. She also explained how she came to the decision of asking BDG . . . Meeting went on to discuss cost yardsticks, design, to have couple of different designs and to try and build 2-bedroom town houses instead of flats.

People's ideas about the design were getting a bit less vague. The co-op would be able to have some kind of choice, within the limits imposed by government 'cost yardsticks'. And they would be employing the architect, though CDS would have a lot of the day-to-day dealings with them.

A special sub-committee was set up to consider which architect to appoint. They went through a list of possibles with CDS, and came to an agreed short-list of three that the co-op would interview. Philip Hughes says: 'CDS gave us a list with a rider saying, they'd have the final choice who they'd be prepared to work with. We knew they were firmly on the side of BDG. It was Hobson's choice.'

CDS didn't demand the 'final choice'. But they did say they'd want to feel able to work with whoever the co-op chose. In some ways it was Hobson's choice for CDS too, according to Catherine Meredith: 'BDG were the only architects in town I knew that would be interested in community-based work. Then it was a bonanza (for architects) and nobody wanted to know anything that was above the odds. So it was a question of looking at anybody else who'd work in this bizarre way.'

Nevertheless CDS had expressly said they wouldn't have on the short-list the architect Billy Floyd had talked to in the pub. Steve Cossack: 'My natural instinct was to go for [him] 'cause CDS wouldn't work with him. When they couldn't come up with the suggestions of why they couldn't work with him, my hackles got raised. We were told, on the one hand, it's your choice entirely; on the other, we can't work with him, him or him.'

The eventual short-list consisted of BDG; Robertson Young, who'd designed the Ribblers Lane scheme Kevin liked; and Furber Thomson. Paul Lusk did some sessions on what an architect's work involved, in designing and controlling the building of a 'scheme'. The committee decided on three criteria for the architect:

1 The people must be the ones who tell the architects what should be built.
2 The architect's involvement with the co-operative must be total.
3 The architects act as advisers and scribes (tell us what is and isn't possible and suggest alternatives).

This was stronger stuff than 'making choices'. It was another step in seeking 'power and control' over housing through the co-op. It was startling and 'bizarre': nobody but the very rich, employing their own architect for an individual house, had this kind of control over design.

But beneath the rhetoric, nobody really knew what it meant in practice. One of the architects who came for interview – the Ribblers Lane architect – virtually ruled himself out by his interpretation of what it meant. Paul Lusk says, 'They said, our idea is we design the houses and you hold the pen. He wasn't happy with that.' Kevin Byrne remembers him more sympathetically: 'He wasn't prepared to come to meetings. He'd have done a fucking brilliant job but he wasn't prepared to come along to the people. He was a very shy feller. That doesn't mean he was a bad person.'

That cut the field down to two. It may seem like Hobson's choice in retrospect, but at the time it was a close-run thing. 'They were very impressed with Carl Thompson,' says Paul Lusk. 'Carl Thompson said he could get on site within a year.

We were convinced it would take a lot longer. We didn't know...we were telling them it would take three years. Also we thought it was going to take much longer because it was a co-op.'

But Carl Thompson's experience of new-build housing was slight. BDG's, though, only amounted to two sheltered housing schemes, and the fact that they were being pushed by CDS went both for and against them. Paul Lusk says, 'When they came to make the decision they had a furious row. Only five were allowed to vote on the basis they'd been to all three interviews.'

Stephen Rice remembers the details slightly differently: 'We decided you had to see every firm of architects for you to have a vote. So that's why we chose five people, so there would be a definite vote one way or the other. But only four of us saw all the architects. Needless to say we had a split vote: me and Billy Floyd voting for [Carl Thompson] and Kevin Byrne and Alec voting for BDG. I think it resolved itself by [Kitty] saying she'd seen both of these firms and she thought BDG was better.'

Stephen and Billy felt the others had bowed to CDS pressure. But in fact others remember a turning-point after the formal interview, talking to Carl Thompson in the pub. 'Then we kicked off: "Why are you driving a fucking Lancia?" Then we got into: "Are you married? Where do your kids go to?" – They went to boarding school of course. "So why don't they go the local comprehensive?"'

This is how Billy Floyd recalls it. Paul Lusk, believing he was supposed to further the cause of BDG (he now feels he misunderstood something Catherine Meredith said to him), 'I asked Carl Thompson where his kids went to school. It was a dirty trick. I don't know how far it was a deliberate ploy on my part. They went for BDG by three to two.'

So in May 1978 BDG were taken on as the co-op's architects. The 'commissioning' was only provisional, because the land wasn't yet secured; and it was agreed that they would work for the co-op with day-to-day instructions coming from CDS.

The sub-committee had interviewed the two then partners of BDG, and it was they who came along to their first encounter with the wider co-op membership in Warwick Street. But introduced on that occasion, listening quietly to the talk of how the co-op was going to design its own scheme and the architects were just there to hold the pen, was Bill Halsall, who was to be the job architect.

Bill was of the same generation as Billy and Kevin, in his late twenties, recently married, living in a flat less than a mile from the Weller Streets. He was local – born and brought up in Bootle – and had studied at Liverpool. One project he'd been involved in as a student had been an analysis of the need for a district centre on Park Road, so he knew a little about the area. His housing design experience amounted to two sheltered schemes then under construction.

From the start Bill didn't want to direct things. Partly this was shyness: he didn't want to push himself forward. And partly he remembered another project he'd worked on as a student, working with a community group: 'It was a terraced street. The boundary of a clearance area ran down this street. The people were upset they were breaking up the community in this way.' So he'd helped them to fight clearance, but had ended up uneasy at having manipulated residents: 'We managed to change the councillors' minds but nothing positive got done [to improve the houses]. We achieved very little for a lot of effort and we'd perhaps used people in a bit of a bad way.'

The gulf between those involved and those not involved in the design is illustrated by people's different first impressions of Bill Halsall. To those not involved, 'At first I thought he was just daydreaming. He was very quiet.' Kitty says: 'I thought he was too quiet at the beginning. He was sitting there saying nothing – getting the feel of what we wanted, I suppose.'

To those who got involved in the design he came over just as quietly. Harry Dono says, 'He always seemed very timid to me: Boom, and he'd drop dead.' But what seemed a weakness in the atmosphere of a general meeting was a strength in a small design committee meeting: 'He was great from the very beginning, Bill,' according to Irene. 'I remember the very first meeting, he was just sitting there, listening to us.'

This was a pretty unfamiliar kind of professional. Kevin Byrne, anxious about whether he'd done the right thing in voting – against his partner in crime, Big Bird – for BDG, felt an immediate liking. 'Soon as we met Bill Halsall I knew he was the guy for me. The others, they weren't our type. He knew the score, I thought, "Yeh, gonna get along good." He was born and bred in the area, only lived locally in a flat, went to work on a bike. I said to him, "Why don't you have a car?" He said, "I live in the area, I only need a bike." Bill being an architect and me being on the buildings we knew what each other was talking about. He radio'd in on me.'

Bill didn't know much of what he was letting himself in for. For the firm his work was 'at risk', so his work wasn't going to be paid for, it was 'his own time'. But he was going along on behalf of the firm. 'I only knew there was this group of people who wanted to form a co-op to get out of their houses. I got hardly any briefing at all, then I was into these meetings trying to do the best I could.'

'I was told later,' Bill recalls, 'that Weller Streets' initial reaction to me was, they'd seen the organ grinder: now here's the monkey.' The monkey found himself, because of the sub-committee plan drawn up by Paul Lusk and Stephen Rice, pitched into three evening meetings a week. On Monday the management committee met; on Tuesday, the 'Outside', to talk about the layout of the scheme; on Wednesday the 'Inside', to talk about the interior of the houses. He says, 'This thing of Inside and Outside was pre-ordained . . . I tended to have to explain the interior stuff to the Outside, and the layout stuff to the Inside.'

Bill had got hardly any briefing because nobody really had a clue how it was going to work. 'It was all a bit confused. My attitude tended to be that I was prepared to discuss what they were interested in rather than structure it. From previous experience with other groups I was very keen to maintain a level of interest....I was trying to get at what they were thinking about and they were going to tell me what was uppermost in their minds first. So we spent an awful lot of time talking about bins.'

The Inside Committee had keen but totally inexperienced people on it, the hard-core being Billy Odger, Irene Stead and Margaret Hughes. Billy Odger, faced with plans of house interiors, found it 'hard, understanding them. I'd never done anything like that myself. Bill Halsall explained the plans.' Margaret says that early on 'Bill was more educating us: about Parker Morris standards; learning how much space we could have per person.'

Meeting them a few times, Bill realized he'd have to take it slowly: explaining that the scheme would have to be to the same Parker Morris standards as Council housing; showing what plans meant. Anyway, as he says, 'It was more difficult for them to make progress till some kind of an idea had come out of the other committees.'

A questionnaire committee, chaired by Kitty Heague, was out interviewing members to establish exactly how many there were, and who wanted what. Fifty-seven people, of the original seventy-six, had bought shares when the books were closed on 8 June. Neither design committee could make much of a move till they knew who they were designing for.

But in addition the Inside was, Bill says, 'more of a passive group'. The Outside was more active from the first. Kevin may say that he was reluctant to chair the committee – he says Billy had said, 'Byrnesy, you'll be chairman of the Building Committee' and explained to others, ''cause he's in building, at least he knows a bit' – but as soon as the meetings began he was anxious to press on Bill Halsall his enthusiasm for Ribblers Lane. The Outside looked at Paul's slides: Kevin pointed out the close he liked, and they talked about the 'village' feeling of the place.

'It wasn't a hard committee,' says Kevin, 'it was easy, 'cause people knew what they wanted.' Pat Russell was confident; Arthur Roberts quiet; Harry Dono – 'on the Outside, I grasped that all right, 'cause, like, I'd worked on the building, and Kevin. You could vision what the outside'd be like.'

The sub-committees reported weekly to the management committee. Billy Floyd recalls: 'At first I used to go to all of them. I sort of acted as co-ordinator for it all the time: so although we used to have reports from all the sub-committees, I used to go to as many as I could so I could confirm it or broaden it out....It seemed a good way of stabilizing everything. Once they got away I stuck with the Outside Layout.'

Bill, trying to get to know all the personalities and understand what they wanted, got a plan of the Miles/Byles site for the Outside. 'It's not much of a site, that's why they gave it to us,' Billy Floyd said to a *Guardian* reporter researching a feature at the time. To one side there were shabby shops on Park Road; then the Byles Street walk-up flats; then, at the top of a slight slope, the gaunt building of the Kodak photographic works; on the fourth side, the single-storey pre-fab that housed the local dole office. The committee talked about the site and what it looked out on to. Two planners came along with a 'draft brief'. Peter Tyrrell, who was also coming along occasionally to the Outside, says, 'They fucking wanted it, 'cause they seen it was different and it was fucking good. There was fear at seeing those two...planners: but as soon as they'd seen it, they were made up.'

'It' was more the way of working than anything on paper at that stage, but the idea of the closes was raised and liked. While the Outside, pushed forward by the nucleus of men, ran ahead, the Inside worked slowly at first. Bill persuaded them to meet only fortnightly till something clearer came out of the Questionnaire and the Outside: but not before they'd concluded the talk about bins by deciding to recommend that 'kitchens and bins should be at the back of the house.'

A trip was arranged for a Sunday. Not just people on the design committee, but anyone in the co-op interested, could come on the coach to look at the housing schemes Paul Lusk had shown slides of. Harry Dono: 'We got a bus one day and we took anyone who wanted to go up to Murdishaw in Runcorn, and they were built on the lines of courts and you had a lot of landscaping. Then we went to Ribblers Lane. That was when it came to the idea, you could have a court and run your car up inside the court.'

This was to be the first of many trips out. Bill says, 'There was a lot of comment generated by bus trips. They found the trips stimulating. They always managed to get into somebody's house. There was feedback from that. You could go for a trip and the grapevine in the area was so strong that within a week you'd have a kind of distilled essence . . . Usually Kitty or Irene would have a pretty good idea of what people thought.'

On that first trip a lot of people were impressed with the pensioners' flats they saw. Lily Faulkner remembers: 'When we went on the trips we saw where the flats had their own front door.' These were flats that looked like houses, with their own gardens too. Harry recalls, 'Funnily enough, the day we went up there, the nicest thing we saw was that pensioner's flat.' Word went round: maybe you didn't have to have all the flats in a block, that you could tell were flats from the outside.

But the crucial thing, as far as moving the design forward was concerned, was the 'close' or 'court' Kevin had pressed everyone to see. Bill had already come to feel that 'Kevin was very much the instigator as far as design was concerned . . . It quickly became apparent that Kevin was a guy with a certain amount of vision. He could visualize things in three dimensions a lot quicker than most people could. He was good at sparking off ideas.'

Kevin wasn't, though, the first one to start drawing the design. Bill had brought along some 'acetate overlays': plastic sheets you could put over a plan of the site and draw on. He invited the Outside to try and draw the Ribblers Lane courts on the Miles/Byles site. As Billy Floyd recalls: 'Pat Russell was the first one to start drawings on the paper 'cause he was hard-faced and he didn't feel embarrassed. I suppose at the time he was like a starter motor on a diesel engine, here you are like. So it went off with a bang right away.'

Other people had a go. They tried to repeat the courtyard across the site. Bill says, 'We got to three and a half of them and we ran out of space. It became immediately obvious that, just trying to repeat that, you weren't going to get all the members on the site.'

Bill started interrogating them about what it was they liked about the Ribblers Lane courts. Recalling the visit, 'I said, this is the one you like. And everybody said, no, I don't like this and I don't like this. There was a fairly narrowly ramped entrance. There was about eight houses. There was a very intimate scale . . . It had garages in it.' There were different materials: brick and timber cladding to the houses: the roofs of the houses were at different levels. It wasn't these factors they liked either. Kevin: 'It was the scale of the whole thing. You felt like being in a mews. We said, "There's something missing here." It was fucking landscaping. We said, "Bill, imagine a wheelbarrow over there and a load of plants."'

Discussion spilled over into Wilkie's after the meeting. Bill tended to order orange juice. When it wasn't his round he tended to get an 'afghan': orange juice laced with vodka. As he remembers it now: 'What you were saying was, you liked the scale of it. It took a lot of questioning and talk to get that . . . If I'd come to the meeting and started talking about scale and proportion, you'd have reacted to that, wouldn't you?'

So the Outside began to work on smaller courts that might still have the feeling of Ribblers Lane. The *Guardian* feature came out on 10 July, while the Outside were in the midst of this: 'The Architects, good luck to them, seem as if they are going to be asked to plan semi-detached houses grouped in small inward looking closes, at the sort of density normally achieved these days by rows of terraces.'

Billy Floyd says they stuck with the courts partly because of feedback from the general membership. 'They didn't want to live in terraced blocks, put it that way, 'cause they associated that with slums. They wanted something detached or semi-detached and that was the nearest we could give 'em.'

The Inside committee was also making comparisons with the houses members lived in. More cautiously, they'd begun to draw their own ideas. Irene says of Bill: 'He wouldn't suggest nothing to us, he'd just draw a square. He'd let us all do our own first. We got a plan of the houses we had then, and worked on that. And then he'd draw something.' Bill had started off with metric 'grids': squares to give people the scale they were drawing at. But that confused people. 'The way round that eventually was to use all the plans gridded in foot squares: a foot is very nearly 300 millimetres, you see.' Billy Odger was surprised at the comparison of the old and the potential new: 'Then, when we got into it and knew the size of the rooms you could have and the Parker Morris style – they didn't look that big to me. Like the living-rooms, they were only about 18 inches bigger than Peckie [Pecksniff Street].'

But they'd have a hall; more kitchen–dining space; more bedrooms; and toilets and bathrooms. The drawings were all still tentative. By mid-July, though, the design committees knew who they'd be catering for: the questionnaire committee had finished their work.

Kitty says she chaired the questionnaire committee because: 'Why the committee asked me, I was like Billy: I knew everybody, everybody knew me. They decided I'd know if anybody was telling a lie.' The group consisted of women: Kitty, Irene, Ann Byrne, Ann Ford, Ann Caddis and Vera Rietdyke. It had been generally agreed that the women would be better than the men at asking questions on the doorstep or in the back kitchen. Besides, Kitty says, the men, apart from Steve Cossack, were never great ones for going round knocking on doors: they were more for meetings or debates in the pub.

The Questionnaire Group's brief was to establish how many of the original seventy-six 'members' were still interested in the co-op, and to work out the sizes of houses and flats they needed: the 'dwelling mix' which the design committees needed. 'It was', says Kitty, 'CDS's idea for us to get a dwelling mix. So we went to Martine's flat: we had our own little meetings, the questionnaire committee. Martine had two bits of paper. Out of that we picked all the questions we needed.'

It was a very detailed questionnaire, including things like, 'How many electric points do you have?' 'How many would you like to have?' The committee assumed Martine knew what she was doing; Martine wanted to cover all the angles.

'We decided', Kitty recalls, 'to split up into twos and do so many different streets of the people who were interested in the co-op. We went through the questions and we filled out the forms.' The doorstep questioning took two nights, then the group met Martine again to go through the forms. Martine took them away and soon returned with a set of index cards with family details on them.

Much of the information was very elaborate (and was never, in the event, used). But the basic information about who wanted and needed what size of property was vital. And there were a few problems with that. 'There were only two or three telling a little white lie,' says Kitty, 'saying their grandson lived with them to get a two-bedroomed flat, when they didn't. I think it was because of the Corpie: they did that with [applying to] them. They didn't need to with us.'

It was hard for people to get used to the idea of 'your own', making decisions about what sort of place you got. People were used to dealing with 'them', the Corpie, where you did your best to maximize your points. A lot of emphasis was placed on the 'confidentiality' of the information: the one advantage of the Corpie was, they didn't know you. By and large the co-op took their lead from the Corporation way of doing things in catering for need: HOUSING FOR NEED NOT FOR GREED was a slogan Billy had coined to describe what they were after. Kitty: 'At the time we had a couple of young girls not married who had a baby. If they'd gone to the Corporation they'd have got a flat. What we looked at was the future: they were old enough to be married and have more. So that's why they got a three-bedroomed house which they'd never have got off the Corporation.'

Otherwise the number of bedrooms people got corresponded to their need.* The sensitive subject was flats. As the Questionnaire committee's report said: 'The proposed dwelling mix provides flats only to people who expressly stated a flat was acceptable. The number of bedrooms in flats corresponds to the co-op members' *wishes*.'

Armed with the dwelling mix CDS now sought, and got, confirmation that the Corporation wouldn't take up any 'nomination rights' – the deal Catherine Meredith had swung over a glass of Christmas cheer the previous December.

The design committees now had a firm basis to work on. There was, though, a lingering uncertainty about 'flats'. Just after the interviewing had been done, Bill Halsall had had to give an assurance about this: 'The Architects discussed what

---

* The dwelling mix arrived at was sixteen flats and forty-five houses. Six flats were to be one-bedroomed (1B); ten flats 2B. Of the houses, six were to be 2B; thirty-two 3B; seven 4B. At first there were smaller and larger sizes within the same number of bedrooms, but this was eliminated later to reduce the number of different house types.

'flats' actually meant, no higher than 2-storey with own front door.'

This corresponded with the Outside's views at a meeting just before that, in late June: 'It was agreed that a number of 2-storey flats might need to be included and if so they should be incorporated within the houses.'

Flats were going to be needed to get all the members on the site: but even those people Kitty and the others on the Questionnaire committee had established would take flats, were apprehensive about what that might mean. Including the flats among the houses led to two complications. Higher standards, and some additional things like alarms, could be included if the flats were 'sheltered': but sheltered flats were normally in a block on their own. Bill Halsall brought it up at an Inside meeting in late August:

> Bill Halsall asked about the reaction of the elderly people to 'sheltered housing'. Kitty Heague said that the general feeling, as reflected in the questionnaire results, is not in favour of sheltered housing. Bill Halsall wondered if the wrong feeling about sheltered housing had been presented. Kitty Heague said nobody had been particularly interested in learning anything else about it.

There was a special meeting of the Inside with Kitty and the elderly there. There was a second problem to sort out too. 'We asked the pensioners, did they mind living on the top or would they live on the bottom?' Too many wanted the ground floor: there had to be an equal number of ground and first floor, if the flats were to be mingled in with the houses. So, Kitty says, 'We called them in . . . Then we had to sort them out: anyone with medical reasons why they couldn't go into the top flats.' The balance was sorted out, though there remained 'one person we told she should live on the bottom. She said, "I won't live on the bottom, I'd be scared."'

As for the sheltered issue, as it was reported back to the

Outside committee: 'What emerged from discussion is that the old people would like to live next to some of their older friends, but not in a large group of old people.'

Meanwhile, from July to September, the design committees pressed decisively forward. At the centre of this was a growing friendship and rapport between Bill Halsall and Kevin Byrne. Billy Floyd thinks 'it was because Kevin was in the fucking [building] game and Bill understood how hard he had to work for his fucking living. Kevin never went into it thinking he was inferior to Halsall; and Halsall accommodated it.'

Kevin says, 'Bill'd leave it to me to lead into the others.' It wasn't a two-man show, though: Peter Tyrrell's view is 'I think Kevin led it for a while. He brought the best out of a lot of other people. He did lead them into a lot of other things. They started to produce a lot of things themselves.'

Kevin had fixed on the Ribblers Lane court as the idea to work from. 'It was Floydie and my idea. We never moved from that. We said that to Halsall. We stuck to it.' He and Billy used to take Ann and Thelma out there. 'That used to be like a haven, on the summer nights, to go to Ribblers Lane. "This is it, Byrnesy." "Yeh, this is it, Billy."'

The Outside worked at ways of getting the feeling of 'scale', of the 'village'. They tried out the idea of a village green in the middle, with houses radiating out from it, and a bloody great wall round the whole thing. Bill Halsall didn't quite know whether they were joking or not. Kevin: 'We all wanted to leave them streets; get down here; surround ourselves with a fucking wall and gun-turrets. We'd lived in that shite, we wanted to protect ourselves . . . We did say that. It was all done in jest, but it was all said.'

Bill pointed out that 'as soon as you have a wall, you get people wanting to get over it'. They began to look at ways of making the scheme uninviting to outsiders without a wall: screening with trees, houses not looking directly out on to Miles Street or Byles Street, low walls. The idea persisted.

Harry Dono reported for the Outside to the first Annual General Meeting in mid-August; he 'described the progress on alternative designs which have been based very much on small closes and on an inward-looking design'.

By late August the Inside committee had graduated to drawing possible house types for the scheme. Margaret Hughes says it grew from when Bill 'gave us a load of designs that could be shuffled round in the basic four walls. He used to give us pieces of paper to try and design how we thought, how we liked it. Bill'd get a big sheet and start drawing and say, "What d'you think of that?"'

To get kitchens, living-rooms and gardens on the back – as the Inside felt most people wanted – they had to work from a more or less square house 'shell'. Within that, Irene Stead says, Bill 'never used to push ideas on you. He'd spend hours; and yet he'd always get his own way. It was always your idea there, but changed. He'd never say, "That's wrong, you're doing that wrong."' Irene herself, like Billy Odger and Margaret, found herself getting more and more interested in what they were doing. According to Kevin, 'Irene put a lot of work into it by being a fucking nit-picking person.' Bill says, 'She started off as the one who was always going to ask the awkward question or complain.' That in itself encouraged others: she was as unembarrassed in her questions as the 'starter motor' of the Outside committee, Pat Russell, had been in putting pen to paper.

The ideas were coming together. Out of the idea of a 'fight', out of anger and frustration, the co-op had in principle got itself a site. Now, through the design, Kevin thinks, 'The co-op's idea of itself was being born. No one had a fucking idea what a co-op was. As the design went along the co-op matured.' And a way of going about the design was being discovered too. Bill Halsall recalls:

'In the design meetings, and in the pub after, an awful lot of ideas were thrown around. In discussing design that automatically led on to discussing how you're going to live: a sort of idealized society – a political discussion, a housing management discussion. We weren't just talking about the design. Design very quickly blurred into how you're going to live in the inner city. So that, when the idea came together, it was coming together partly as a physical design, but partly as a physical embodiment of all these other things that had been talked about.'

The ideas weren't coming together in cosy agreement. 'When there was an issue,' Bill says, 'they went at it hammer and tongs until it got resolved.' He remembers 'Kevin and Harry Dono arguing about things: about one kind of courtyard layout against another kind'. But the basic idea of the courtyard persisted. Kevin says, 'The idea of the design was to make the courts, to make them intimate, packed away, every one the same, no one having more.'

Everyone having the same had become a persistent idea. 'It got to the point where everybody had to have an equal share of the sunlight cake,' says Bill: they worked on ways in which all the houses could face south or east to achieve this. It was partly an egalitarian idea, growing out of the idea of the co-op, and out of the feeling of 'neighbourliness' of the old streets. But it was also a practical necessity. Half the co-op was related to somebody else in the co-op. Two-thirds of committee members had a relative among the general membership. Philip Hughes: 'We used to find it was a terrible problem. You had to look to be fair. It couldn't be houses for the boys or the girls.'

The idea of the elderly being mixed in with the rest was a similar mixture of idealism and pragmatism. Younger people felt the elderly should be cared for within the community. And the elderly themselves didn't want to be split off, as Kevin says: 'The old ones who lived in the terraces next door to their families: it came very much from them.'

These ideas weren't on paper, as ideas: they were woven into the minutes of meetings, expressed in the different drawings people had come up with. Bill Halsall was beginning to feel himself out on a limb. He'd go to CDS and find that their view was, 'You form a co-op to give people a lot of individual choice. I was coming back and saying, they don't want that, they all want the same. It didn't make me very popular.'

Bill Halsall had been to meeting after meeting for three months, by early September. In that time various different CDS staff had been to different meetings: none of them as consistently as Bill, so they weren't in as close touch with the way ideas were developing. In theory it had been intended to be the other way round, with CDS staff taking more of the initiative, as Paul Lusk had written to the co-op on 5 June:

> BDG's role in this process is to define what facts and opinions they require and to produce a sketch scheme in accordance with a brief which will be prepared by CDS in consultation with the co-op. The burden of day-to-day contact with the co-op should be borne by CDS, with the Architects' presence being requested at meetings only when it is definitely felt to be necessary. All requests involving work or presence from the Architects must go through CDS who will pass them on to BDG as formal instructions.

None of this had happened. In early September Catherine Meredith said at a management committee meeting, as the minutes record:

> CDS have been requested by architects for a written brief, because they have not received any formal instruction. Although good discussion has taken place at sub committee level, there is a need for some back tracking.

Bill Halsall himself wanted some more formal statement of what the design was about; and Catherine Meredith and the partners in BDG wanted to see on paper what was happening. It was agreed that the design committees would begin to work on a brief with Bill, and with Martine and myself from CDS (which I'd recently joined).

This took place against the background of recent arguments between the committee and CDS about CDS's role and what CDS were getting paid. Relations were a bit strained. And although, at a joint meeting of the Inside and Outside in late September, 'Martine Gouilleux suggested that it was important to get away from the...sketch schemes so that the group could produce the design principles', it wasn't as easy as that: the 'principles' were in the sketches; the arguments came about over different sketches and designs, not over abstract ideas.

Within the design committees, in September, the question of the brief didn't seem that important. Controversy had started to build up over the three different house types the Inside had drawn up. Within the square shell, they'd produced three different downstairs layouts: a through lounge and back kitchen; a kitchen–dining-room and separate living-room; and three separate rooms, living, kitchen and dining. Argument about this spilled over into the management committee. Kitty says, 'I can remember Kevin saying, They're all going to be the same. If you start asking, do they want this, they're going to want too bleeding much, Kevin was always saying.'

Kevin was anxious about the 'ideal' of sameness; and that too many different house types would make the scheme costly to build. Against that Kitty supported Irene: 'I agreed with doing the different house types but not too many. Irene was the one for that, 'cause Irene had a lot of arguments on the design. She was saying, "The men don't understand, it's the women who are in the house all the time."'

Irene 'came out of herself in the process of design', in Bill Halsall's view. 'She could put her finger on problems with the design.' Bill felt that the square house shell could give room for choice between the different internal layouts. 'My position became to persuade people that some could have one, others could have others.'

Irene stuck to her guns, supported by Billy Odger. She'd moved on from being 'nit-picking': 'She'd find fault but after a while you'd see reasons why she did find fault,' is Peter Tyrrell's assessment. 'Some men, if they were told they were wrong, they disappeared. But not Irene . . . She stood up to it all and produced some good stuff.'

Arguments were spilling across the Inside and Outside committees now. Rob Macdonald, who took the minutes of all the meetings, says that at first, 'The question was, how could the women who wanted to talk about the inside things get on in the same meeting with the men? It's easy to say, think about the inside of the houses at the same time as the fact that you'll be overlooked by flats in Byles Street, but in practice it's hard.' But now people on the design committees were seeing, in practice, the links between the problems. For instance, the Inside were working on the assumption that kitchens should be at the back. This clashed with what the Outside were doing. It came up at the management committee:

> Steve Rice . . . said that 98% of the co-op had expressed the desire for kitchens at the back. The outside sub committee have been working towards approx two-thirds kitchens at the front. How was this to be resolved and explained to the body of the co-op at the general meeting?

The Outside were doing it to get sunlight in the living-rooms at the back, and to avoid living-rooms being overlooked by the Byles Street walk-up flats. But it wasn't satisfactory. The two committees agreed to merge. Irene says 'the Outside was more or less worked out as the Inside was coming into more: so they came into one.' Philip Hughes adds: 'If truth be known, one or both of them was getting poorly attended.'

The low attendance at design committee meetings was a perennial problem. The small groups had originally been intended to encourage more people to get involved; but the result had merely been a shuffling of the pack of committee members. If you hadn't been involved at the beginning, the design groups were hard to break in on. I had first-hand experience of this: going along intermittently as a CDS worker, I found it hard to understand what people were talking about or where they were up to.

There had been feedback from the general membership through the bus trip, and the questionnaires, and the grapevine. In addition, Billy Floyd recalls, there were 'people meeting in the streets and mumbling and there was all kinds of meetings of people who turned up at those sorts of meetings with a fucking spokesman. And they'd turn up, to make sure it was all getting done above board and nobody was getting anything forced on them.'

But that wasn't felt to be enough. Stephen Rice, who with Dickie Sharp was leading the 'Education Committee' at this time, felt particularly concerned that the committee were becoming 'élitist'. 'So I tried – failed miserably – to get everybody involved. And don't forget we had a lot of education, information coming in. And that made us more élitist. The gap widened.'

Stephen produced information sheets for each general meeting in the form of a newsletter. Pressure from him helped to get the committee to decide they'd have a general meeting on 28 September to talk about the design. At the management committee that prepared for this meeting: 'Billy Floyd explained the need for greater involvement of the body of the co-op, and he thought this meeting would be the first of many.'

It was agreed that committee members would explain what they'd been doing to the membership, and try to get feedback. Margaret Hughes remembers her nervousness at presenting where the Inside were up to. She'd never spoken at a meeting before. Even though they'd had a rehearsal, she found the words wouldn't come out right when all the faces were there in front of her. As she recalls what she managed to get over: 'We said, "We've got so many different house types:

pick your own." We'd had about six house types, then we'd dwindled it down to three so it wouldn't get too complicated. Once the people realized – the people could pick what they wanted.'

In fact that issue of choice was still controversial. This meant that, as Billy Floyd said at the subsequent post-mortem on the general meeting, there were 'too many people speaking with slightly different points of view, i.e. people on the committees.' Actually that didn't go down altogether badly with the membership. One recalls, 'They were arguing with themselves. And they were the ones running it,' with a note of approval in her voice.

But too much had been expected of the meeting; just as Steve Cossack at the very first meeting which had talked about a co-op had tried to compress a lot of learning into a little space, so the design committees did the same. They started talking about 'controlled aspect' houses, in architectural jargon, when trying to explain how the houses and flats wouldn't look on to the the Byles Street flats.

And the gulf between the committees and the membership was confirmed. 'They were the ones running it.' The committees had got involved in the *ideas* behind the design: it came over to the general membership as being able to 'pick what they wanted'. Sammy Roberts felt it impressed the members that the co-op was a real, important organization: 'When we got the architects in and started showing them the designs of how it was going to be, people saw: "They must have some pull here, they're even getting architects along and telling them what to do. And they're doing it; they're designing their own."'

The majority of people who attended general meetings were women. Their reactions supported the idea of a range of choice of house types that Irene and the others on the Inside had been pushing. Here's an extract from the minutes to illustrate the level of debate:

Question: Are we going to have one kind of house? Some feeling from the floor suggested that it is not possible to provide the different types of house that has been suggested from the information so far presented.

The broad answer to this question was, no, there is a little scope for variety of house type.

Question: If we were going into a corporation house, what kind of space standards would the houses be based upon?

The answer to this question, was, no difference, because both corporation and the houses for the Weller Streets have to be designed to the Parker Morris standards.

Question: What kind of choice, if any, would we have if we were going into a corporation house?

The broad answer given to this question was, no choice, in fact the most important difference between the Weller Streets and the corporation tenant is that the member of the Weller Streets co-operative does have a choice.

There wasn't any objection to the basic idea of 'equality'; but people thought some degree of 'choice' ought to be possible, otherwise how would the co-op be different from the Corporation? The committee tacitly accepted that point of view, while remaining committed to the original idea of the co-op 'controlling' the design. The co-op was operating on two levels: the committee involved in the 'co-op idea', the general membership in it for a house: the committee would try to develop ways of getting the general members' views and ideas incorporated in what they did.

So, in October and November, the Inside/Outside and Education committees joined forces to hold small group meetings, including the wider membership, where information could be exchanged in a more informal setting. Billy Lybert, a general member, recalls those smaller meetings in the Labour rooms in Admiral Street: 'We decided to have smaller meetings, by the house types. If it wasn't feasible, what you were asking for, Bill Halsall, he'd tell you. You couldn't get that with the Corpie.'

A much simpler questionnaire than the original one was used at the meetings. After explanations, then discussions in groups of four or five, people were asked to complete it. Kitty says, 'Say, we called all the three-bedroomed house people in. They got more out of them, about what they wanted. It was at them meetings they were saying, "D'you want a through lounge, three rooms or a kitchen–diner?"...When they had the meetings with the group, a couple of them started to make up their minds properly. They were explaining the sun 'll always be on the living-room end of your house and all that.'

These meetings confirmed the general support for the ideas the design committees had worked on: small closes, containing six houses or so; flats among the houses; gardens, kitchens and bins at the back, where most sunlight should fall if possible; and no one having to look out on to the Byles Street flats, the photographic works or the shabby shops on Park Road if possible. And people enjoyed the meetings too. Lily Durrant, a pensioner member: 'When they started drawing the plans it was lovely. He'd say, "What d'you think of these ideas?" He'd bring the drawings along: we'd all give different views and different ideas.'

'They all expected massive things,' says Billy Odger. 'We tried to explain to them.' The size of the rooms in the proposed houses had shocked him at first; he passed on the knowledge he'd acquired. The arguments about whether or not to have different house types were resolved by popular feeling for the different options, and the fact that these could be accommodated within the same basic 'shell'. Originally there'd been, as Bill Halsall recalls, 'a through-lounge lobby – led by Irene and Kitty – and a kitchen–diner lobby. Kevin was the leader of the kitchen–diner lobby.' Ironically, when it came to making his own choice, Kevin changed his mind. Having specialized in the Outside's work, he had to go through the same learning

Billy Odger and Margaret and Irene had gained about the Inside. 'When I got the plans I was doing all the measurements. Near enough it was the same size of [living-] room we had then, in Micawber Street. So I changed my mind, I went for the through lounge. Certain snides have remembered, "Oh, Byrnesy changed his fucking tune."'

This consultation with the wider membership involved broadening the kinds of information available. Bill Halsall did artist's impressions as well as drawings. A group of the Inside/Outside got together in October/November to make a model of the site and the house shells to fit on it. They went down to BDG's office. Bill Halsall recollects: 'That happened on Sunday morning which always ended up at the pub at lunchtime. It was a much more relaxed session . . . Psychologically that was a help: quite a lot of people got involved in it.'

The model was used to inform general members of proposals, and for the Inside/Outside themselves to experiment with the design. Billy Floyd says there were 'endless permutations of little fucking wooden blocks and thousands of little drawings about the way the blocks were facing and where the entrances were on the roads and you couldn't have an entrance to one of the courts too close to the corner of Byles Street and...' Opinions vary about the usefulness of the model. For committee members, Billy feels, 'I don't think it was an awful lot of use. No, we spent more time making it to scale . . . But for people who've only got a rudimentary grasp, I mean, how many people can understand a two-dimensional drawing? – The model was invaluable in that. There was this camera with a periscope in it: like you were standing in the courtyard.' On the other hand, Margaret Hughes, although by now experienced in working with plans, says of the model: 'It was like a big tortoise. You could see what it was going to be like.'

Meanwhile Martine was pushing the committee to keep working on the brief – she in turn being pushed by Catherine Meredith. She produced drafts which the committee commented on. It was largely a question of getting down on paper what had already been talked about. Discussion tended to get a bit squeezed by other matters: the group meetings with general members, experiments on the model. Nevertheless a draft was completed by December.

In October CDS sent to the Housing Corporation, on the co-op's behalf, their application for approval to buy the land. An early sketch drawing went with it, of culs-de-sac. This and the writing of the brief went on against a background of some friction with CDS: after the general meeting of 28 September the committee were anxious to keep general interest up, were looking for ways to involve the wider membership, and were nervous of delays in progressing the paperwork. So they put the pressure on CDS.

Through this process the committee members were gaining in confidence all the time. One example of this was when a housing association architect came along to give a 'training session' on design. He unrolled his plans. The design committees, with six months' experience behind them now, examined them carefully. 'That's a drawing of a lot of roads,' said one member. It was a conventional estate design: it wasn't what the Weller Streets members wanted for themselves. The housing association architect rolled up his plans.

The co-op's design planned to have the minimum of road, with one main access road, and cobbles in each courtyard which would double as car parking surface and pedestrian way. They began to glimpse, seeing the housing association architect, how far they'd travelled in five months of design work and, indeed, in the year and a half since the co-op had begun. None of them had imagined they'd be designing houses for the community – themselves and their relatives, neighbours and friends. Now they could understand and criticize the ideas behind a design. 'They just gave him an architectural crit on this scheme,' says Bill Halsall of the architect's visit. 'They criticized his layout in terms he could understand. I don't think he's ever recovered.'

By December they were developing still further the idea of the 'village'. They began to think about ways of landscaping the site with trees and shrubs to get the feeling they were after: to add on what the original Ribblers Lane court had clearly been missing. The ideas were coming together. Bill Halsall recalls the cover of the first Annual Report: 'Under a picture of the site Stephen Rice has written: "Just a barren site at present: we will turn it into an oasis in the desert." There was the ideas about, say, landscape, that they wanted lush landscape – a rural village in the heart of Liverpool – birdboxes and so on. On a more practical level they were talking about a scheme with urban qualities: it's formal urban squares really, rather than a village street or something...'

Small wonder that to the general membership the leading members were seen as 'dreamers'. But they were determined too. 'That was all the conversation,' says the disgruntled wife of one leading member. 'That's all they'd talk about. They were power-struck.' Bill Halsall says, 'Kevin was just completely nuts about the whole thing. It was obsessive. I think we were all obsessed with it.' And that urge for a 'fight' that had motivated some of the men from the beginning made them aggressive, even arrogant now that they felt they knew what they were doing. They felt they knew enough to tell the professionals where to get off.

But underlying the aggression was still unease: unease at how much the general members were involved; unease at the fact that they still didn't own the land; unease that the professionals still always seemed to look cleverer than them, however much they knew; unease that nobody in authority had yet given an OK to their ideas. Bill Halsall felt it too: 'On a rational basis you'd probably think, it's a bit dicey, this. It was necessary to believe.' Bill was out on a limb too. And there was, according to Paul Lusk, a sense that 'if people knew what they were up to, they'd be smashed: there was this sense of being party to the conspiracy.'

Some events around this time made them feel suspicious. The discussions over the brief, in particular, had been puzzling. Martine had kept trying to pull them back from the actual drawings, to the 'principles'. Billy Floyd recalls, 'She kept getting these books out and getting these plans out. I remember one meeting she said, "Let's look at this idea."' And Bill Halsall felt uneasy: 'Being able to deliver the goods was the real test.' How sure could they be that Bill could deliver the goods?

Bill Halsall wasn't that experienced. The confidence the co-op had developed in him wasn't based on any knowledge of how he'd deal with bureaucrats or builders: central parts of the architect's job. He was learning along with them. 'We knew something was going on,' Kevin says. Inevitably the senior partners in BDG, and Catherine Meredith at CDS, felt nervous about Bill's ability to cope. And the courtyard design looked 'rigid'. Billy Floyd accepts 'If you look at a plan view of the site, it looked like a load of block houses.'

Derek Hindle of BDG, working from the draft brief and the few co-op meetings he'd been along to, drew up an alternative design over the Christmas holiday. CDS and BDG discussed it. Bill Halsall recalls: 'I got this phone call from Martine. She said, "You've seen this design from Derek, what do you think of it?" What I said was, "Go ahead. If they want it, they can have it: as long as the scheme is judged on its own merits by the Weller Streets."'

Derek brought along his alternative to the management committee in early January. 'We thought,' Billy Floyd says of their own scheme, 'they're not going to wear this 'cause it looks so fucking bland. It looks like an army barracks.' When Derek brought out the plan and explained it, Kevin says, 'We were a bit hurt that night, we were a bit taken aback. They were only terraced housing, but just slipped back to give a hint of privacy. It wasn't what we were working on. We were working on a courtyard.'

'Slipped' was the key word. As Billy Floyd remembers that night: 'Hindle produced this thing: it was a load of terraces, but they're slipped. And he had a crescent to accommodate about eighteen. We tried to put across to him, they want courtyards. It seemed to us, it had to have BDG's brush marks on the fucking canvas. He didn't seem to see, the fancy pieces, the landscaping and all that, would make it all right.'

Derek's plain-talking manner has, before and since, some-times earned him the respect of co-op members. But that night it was part of what made them feel 'a bit hurt'. As Kevin describes it: 'He said he could produce them off the top of his head. He could do them every day: uniform like that. He came along and didn't like the idea. We called him Rupert the Bear: he had on this aubergine jacket and striped trousers...'

They weren't as aggressive that night as they had been a couple of months before. It took a while for it to sink in. They agreed to consider the idea in the Inside/Outside committee. There it was tried out on the model. It was discussed in the pub. Billy Floyd: 'We talked about it, me and Kevin, and we said, "This is a scheme that looks nice that we don't want."' It was, as Bill Halsall describes it, 'more of a suburban looking scheme with cul-de-sacs, rather than tight little courtyards'. 'What we wanted', Billy Floyd affirms, 'was a village.'

The design committee felt totally committed to the court-yard idea. 'We'd had to chop things off and move it around,' Kevin says. 'In the end we were stuck with this idea.' What actually happened then is a matter of dispute. Billy Floyd says, 'We talked about that for two weeks and then Kevin ripped it up at the Outside Committee. That was at the stage where we were insulting everybody.' Everyone in the co-op says the plans were torn up; nobody remembers doing it themselves.

The idea was torn up anyway, whatever happened to the plans. As Peter Tyrrell saw it: 'I think it was Kevin again, sticking to – It's going to be stupid, it's going to look ridiculous. We could have our original thing with a few fucking changes: we said okay. But there was no way we were going to be foisted with what fucking Hindle wanted.'

Derek's ideas did provoke some minor changes in the scheme: for instance, a problem about pedestrian routes through the site was sorted out. And they did also provoke people into realizing how committed they were to their scheme. As Bill Halsall reflects on it: 'People like Billy Floyd saw it as being professionals, the bad guys trying to pull another stunt. But there was also a reaction of: "It's done us a favour by proving our commitment and understanding of what we do want."'

It had got personalized into 'what Hindle wanted', but behind that was people's commitment to the long process of debate, argument and thought they'd gone through. 'They meant months and months of work by the people themselves, these drawings,' Kevin says. 'And this guy came along: "You know all the work you've been doing for the last six months: fucking sling it." [Bill Halsall] must have felt he was a lackey going to talk to the fucking troops.'

The co-op's ideas were embedded in the drawings, in how they imagined the scheme would look. It wasn't what Bill Halsall wanted: it was what the co-op wanted: his way of working had turned out to be a method of enabling them to express their feelings and thoughts about their community, and the co-op. Rob Macdonald, a witness to all this, says of the design: 'It wasn't the architect's idea. When you think about it, it's a very simple idea: they got the courtyard and they drew it on the site. If you go to Ribblers Lane and look at Ribblers Lane, there's not a lot of physical similarity. They in their mind said, "We like Ribblers Lane, we want Ribblers Lane" – but they haven't got that.' Kevin may describe it as the Japanese trick – 'You know, they steal an idea then make it better than the people who invented it', but in practice Ribblers Lane had been a starting-point for debate which ended up with the Weller Streets' own courtyard in their own layout.

On 17 January 1979 approval came through from the Housing Corporation to buy the land. It was important to press on. 'What happened over January was,' says Bill Halsall, 'it became apparent that the Weller Streets weren't going to be budged. The choices were fairly stark. Eventually the decision was made to back the scheme as it was.'

CDS and BDG accepted the design the co-op had come up with. As Catherine Meredith puts it: 'I guess what I had to face through was, it didn't bloody matter what it looked like. It was egalitarianism: that they did squash everything on because of that.' For the Weller Streets' committee the two things were the same: egalitarianism *was* what it looked like. But now they would have to convince more than just their own paid professionals of the sense and rightness of that. Now they'd have to convince the public bureaucracy as well.

1 The old Weller Streets, now demolished, which used to be a great tourist spot. You could see the cathedral from the outside toilet.

2 From the *Guardian* in 1978: the first piece of journalism to take the Weller Streets seriously.

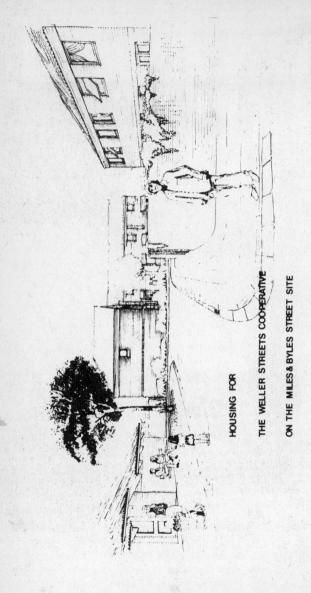

HOUSING FOR

THE WELLER STREETS COOPERATIVE

ON THE MILES & BYLES STREET SITE

3 A drawing that's finally, in 1986, coming true, with the construction of the final courtyard on the left.

4 The courtyard in Ribblers Lane that was an early inspiration for Kevin Byrne, leader of the design committee.

5 Co-op members on the design committee discuss plans.

THIS LAND NOW BELONGS TO THE PEOPLE

6 The sign that showed that the Weller Streets at last owned their own land. Unfortunately, after a few weeks the wall fell down.

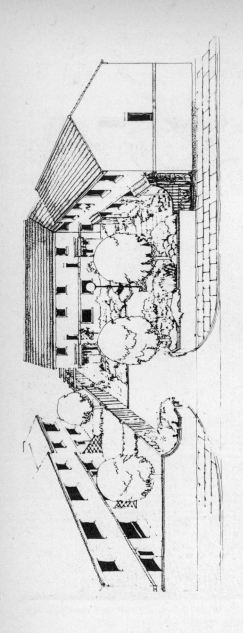

7 Typical courtyard, showing pensioners flats and family houses.

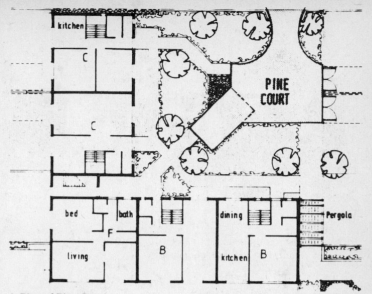

8 Plan of Pine Court.

9 A carnival procession on the way from the old Weller Streets towards the – then still to be built – new estate.

10 A group photo of the co-op on 17 August 1980, when building was about to start, now regarded as 'the team photograph'.

11 Philip Hughes making a point at a packed meeting of the general membership of the co-op.

12

13   14

12–14 Site visits by co-op members during the building work.

15 Arthur Roberts' kitchen–dining room.

16 Moving in.

17 Poplar Court.

18 Hazel Court.

19 Prince Charles visits the Weller Streets.

20 The poem-on-a-plaque whose unveiling marked the completion of the estate.

5

This Land Now Belongs to the People:
Setbacks and Celebrations

It all seems clearer looking back, of course, than it did at the time. It seems only logical to describe the development of the design on its own, as if everything else stopped for nine months.

But everything else didn't. When the design committees were in full flood, in August 1978, the co-op was also negotiating its development agreement with CDS, and organizing its first ever Annual General Meeting. Throughout the design period there were negotiations for the land, fund-raising events, hassles about recording membership attendance and subs, rows with wives and husbands about the amount of time people were sitting in the pub talking about the bloody co-op, an application for a grant for a paid worker...all this made it even more remarkable that the design had progressed so well and so far.

'We thought it was going to take much longer because it was a co-op,' Paul Lusk had said at the time of the architect's appointment, and indeed that's a common criticism from administrators and professionals. All this involving the people is all very well, but it holds up the building of houses.

That wasn't true of the Weller Streets. The design ideas had developed while CDS's negotiations were proceeding to buy the land. It was the negotiations which held up progress. The Council resolved to offer the site in April; but by mid-September the Council were turning down CDS's latest offer.

To CDS this was frustrating but routine. To the co-op it was ridiculous bureaucracy. CDS were challenging the basis on which the City set its price; the co-op's committee was suspicious that CDS were hiding things from them. 'You were always at their mercy,' is how Harry Dono describes the feeling. At a time when the committee was worried about the general members' commitment, the delays seemed intolerable. The programme CDS had drawn up showed a start of building on site in May 1980, nearly two years away. So it would be four years before people could move into new houses.

Throughout October this was the subject of angry and heated debate in the management committee. And besides, if there was a hot political issue involved in the land price, why weren't the co-op being brought into the battle? 'It was a fucking crusade,' says Billy Floyd, 'it was a revolution at the time. We didn't want the same kind of price like Barratt's or Wimpey's. So we were going to make a stand for housing associations...It all went to the wall. This was all contrived with Meredith.'

Catherine Meredith persuaded the co-op to let CDS handle the negotiations a while longer. Finally, in early November, the City officers agreed to recommend to the Council that negotiations proceed on the basis of the original offer of £36,000.

Some of this aggravation was a clash of style and temperament as well as of policy. Since the row over the development agreement in August, Catherine Meredith herself had become the CDS representative, fortnightly, at management committee meetings. There was no personal rapport between her and committee members, particularly the men. She came over as a cool bureaucrat who wouldn't let her guard drop, as others did, in the pub afterwards. In turn they seemed to her a group of men, mostly of her own age, who were engaged in an exciting and innovatory idea, but who on a personal level were traditional in their attitudes to the roles of women and men. So they didn't get on. The men on the committee called her 'the fat cat' behind her back,* and there was a lot of petty nonsense at meetings about whether she could bring up items that weren't on the agenda, or whether her items could be brought forward if she had to leave early. So, in spite of the fact that her customary style of working was similar to the Weller Streets' – among others in housing she had a reputation for being aggressive and unyielding – there wasn't a meeting of minds.

Negotiations for the land weren't over when a price was agreed with the Council. A corner of the site was owned by the Church. The local vicar, Colin Bedford, had originally · wanted the site developed for his own parishioners; an article appeared in the parish magazine hinting that the Weller Streets would never acquire the land.

'The printing of the article is not helping the general morale amongst the co-operative membership,' it was drily noted at management committee. Again the committee wanted to take decisive action. Again Catherine Meredith persuaded them to let CDS do the negotiating. She wrote to higher authority – as one does with the Church – and finally, in January 1979, the Church accepted an offer of £8,000.

At the same time the Housing Corporation approval came through. At last, after nine months, acquisition of the land was in sight. And immediately pressure on the committee increased again. Everyone in the Weller Streets area got a letter from the Corpie saying they proposed to put the area under a Compulsory Purchase Order. It made clearance seem nearer, and the programmed date for starting on site further away.

'DON'T PANIC!' said Stephen Rice's newsletter on the subject. Mixed among the information about the 'CPO' – Compulsory Purchase Order – was some propaganda:

---

*Martine's nickname was 'the French fox'. The only 'professional' who didn't acquire a nickname was Bill Halsall: the co-op called him Bill.

...don't think that the houses will be pulled down shortly. Every indication that we have suggests that it will be at least two years before the Corporation will start to rehouse the people of the area. This is not a rumour or a myth – THIS IS A FACT!

Stephen hadn't been closely involved in the design, but he'd been working hard on 'education', including putting in an application for a grant for the co-op's own worker: 'At one time I was having two meetings a week and producing information sheets and working fifty hours a week – with overtime – elsewhere.'

Another job he'd taken on was sorting out the co-op's auditor. 'We needed a firm of accountants. Martine offered us three, and they were very CDS type. And I said, "I want to find out for myself," and I interviewed eight or ten other firms: to say to them, "Don't wipe our arses for us, we can do it ourselves."' In fact, though, the co-op plumped for CDS's accountants.

Then, in February, Stephen had a bit of a run in with Paul Lusk over the 'education' role, as the minutes record:

> Steve Rice...expressed some concern about arrangements with CDS Education Officer Paul Lusk, and hoped he would be in better health shortly...Steve Rice expressed the view that the Education Programme was being neglected, due to the heavy schedule of Paul Lusk, and he hoped that CDS could provide a better schedule than could be expected.

Paul was beginning to spend more time with other co-ops and less with the Weller Streets' – inevitably, as the Weller Streets became more experienced themselves. But also, as Rob Macdonald puts it, 'Paul Lusk: he was used as, like, the whipping boy. They often thought he was out of place. They didn't like CDS to get the credit for what they did.' And this 'credit' was beginning to rub off on CDS in other ways. Paul Lusk was working with other co-ops now: co-ops partly encouraged by the Weller Streets' example. Soberly considered, people felt Paul was putting a lot into it: Philip Hughes: 'Luskie was all right. He'd go out of his way to get things done for you. He was committed no doubt about it. He was always willing to come along and give any help he could.'

But his 'commitment' was inevitably of a different kind from that of committee members. Billy Floyd feels 'one of the reasons it worked is, we were all in the same fucking shit. I mean, I had three kids in a 2-up 2-down. These professionals: they go home at night.' The 'professionals' – Bill, Paul, Rory – were united by the 'idea' of the co-op. Members weren't united by an 'idea' in the same way. They were united by their situation. For instance, Sammy Roberts kept working on the committee even though he regarded the likes of Billy, Kevin and Steve as 'Communists' because 'We all had to pull our socks up and pull our weight . . . . We had some people coming to meetings, we'd say to them, "You don't realize we can do these things . . ." With always living in the hovels we were doing, I think that's what made us determined: when we seen other people in their own new houses.'

In February Catherine Meredith sought to formalize the co-op's concern about how long things would take by setting up a fortnightly 'programming' meeting on a weekday afternoon in CDS's offices. 'That was always our line,' Steve Cossack says, 'push, push, push. People said things'd take so long and they'd never tell us why.' The 'why' tended to be the inevitable delays of bureaucracy. That was hard to accept when 'programming' wasn't just an academic exercise but a statement of how long committee members would have to withstand the pressure. Billy Floyd says, 'One night a tart was standing at my door with a jam jar full of cockroaches. People expected us in charge of the co-op to be in charge of their own fucking problems – blocked drains, the lot.' The committee were the ones who had to live with the forecasts of how long it'd take. Sammy Roberts: 'We thought we could do this thing. We were promising people we'd have it done in so-and-so time.'

By March there were yet more problems over buying the land. Even though the Miles/Byles site had been cleared years before, the council hadn't sorted out all the compensation to former owners, and hadn't formally closed the roads that weren't there any more. The committee and CDS pressed the solicitor to find a way round the problem.

And they made another stab at a way of involving the general membership. 'They had this need to be an elite,' Catherine Meredith says, but the gulf between the committee and the general membership was something that grew steadily out of circumstances, and which the people 'in charge of the co-op', in Billy Floyd's phrase, were always anxious about. Stephen Rice in particular kept pressing other people on the committee to beware of it. So at the end of March they tried a different format for general meetings.

The subject was the first discussion of the future management of the estate. The Housing Corporation had made it an 'understanding' of approving the purchase of the site that 'The Co-operative will acquaint the Corporation with, and satisfy it as to, its proposals for management of the development once built, before construction commences.'

And the Inside/Outside committee, in pressing on with ideas for landscaping to create the 'village' feeling, had begun to realize that the maintenance of the landscaping was going to be crucial, and required a commitment from the whole membership.

So, as Harry Dono recalls it, 'What we did at one time, we split ourselves up, and we'd ask questions, then the person in front would ask a question.' The committee split up throughout the meeting to try and get rid of the 'us and them' set-up. Philip Hughes: 'We decided to get 'em all in chairs in a circle, like the Knights of the Round Table. Billy never had a chair, he stood in the middle with the papers in his hand. At the time there was a programme on the telly, David Frost International: he'd be all over the place.' So, inevitably, in the meeting somebody piped up: '"Somebody tell David Frost to sit down" – we'd lost the central point: people kept trying to talk to Billy.'

The meeting was a success. Everyone there said they'd help to keep up the landscaping. Everyone there said they'd enjoyed the meeting done that way. But the experiment wasn't repeated. Maybe it was the pressure of other business that put it out of people's minds at the time, for there were the land negotiations to pursue, and the implications of the design to be followed up.

The Inside/Outside, with the principles of the design established, had been following up their earlier work by setting some priorities for the details they wanted. They decided, for instance, to try to get a high level of insulation; to get gas-fired central heating; to look closely at the kinds of wall and railing they could have to achieve the 'intimate', private feeling they were after. And they'd decided to try to deal with two problems together: the co-op's need for a base (they were meeting mainly in the Labour rooms then, but still kept moving meetings around from place to place), and the gaunt building of the photographic works at the top end of the site. They resolved to try to put a 'community centre' next to the photographic works, which would include an office for the co-op and meeting space for the whole area. They applied to the Inner City Partnership for money; they petitioned the area round Miles/Byles for support.

But the main design problem focused around the smallness of the courtyards. Back in June 1978, when they'd first met the planners, the planners' endorsement of the idea had had a condition attached to it: 'it was noted that the highway engineers have specific dimensional requirements with regards to road and pavement layouts'.

In translation, this meant that the engineers might say the roads were too narrow to be 'adopted' by the Council; and that therefore the co-op would be landed with maintaining their own courtyards.

The issue kept bubbling under the surface of the design debate. When the principles had been established, in January 1979, it came up at the Inside/Outside meeting:

> Derek Hindle said that there are two alternative approaches to the problem:
> (i) accept their [engineers'] standards and change the design;
> (ii) that they, city engineers, will change their standards of adoption.

> Opting for the second alternative, Billy Floyd said that both the DOE and the Local Authority would be required to accept new standards.

This was the 'crusading' spirit that had torn up Derek Hindle's own ideas, that was going to sweep all before it. But behind it, again, was unease. Billy Floyd: 'We had this fear at the time. "Unadopted" seemed an awful lot of responsibility to wear.' Harry Dono, in particular, remembered the one blemish on the Council site near Sefton Park everyone had liked when they were looking for land: the unadopted road that ran by it, pitted with ruts and holes. And in the Weller Streets area, Billy recalls, 'There was a lot of unadopted streets around here and those streets were a fucking shambles. I suppose that was in the back of your mind: This is all inferior, this, it's not good enough to adopt.'

Representatives of BDG and CDS went to see the city engineers to see what leeway there was. The result was devastatingly bad. It's worth quoting at length from the city engineers' letter of 7 February, to get an idea of what the co-op suddenly realized they were up against:

> The areas shaded red would not be adopted, maintenance, etc. would therefore have to be carried out by the frontagers. This is very undesirable as the frontagers are unlikely to have the skill, equipment or indeed finance to carry out the necessary work, consequently the areas could well fall into a state of disrepair to

the severe detriment of the housing...Regardless of what
layout is finally obtained for the development, the car parking
areas will not be adopted, it is, therefore, considered to be
essential that car parking space is provided within the curtilage
of the dwellings...The current layout cannot, I consider, be
satisfactorily amended to take account of my comments and I
would, therefore, strongly recommend to you that a fresh
approach be made to the design of this development.

It was hard to penetrate beneath the jargon language:
'frontagers' for people, 'curtilage' for boundaries. And if you
did, what seemed to be underneath was ignorance of and
complete scepticism about a co-op of local people who'd be
'unlikely to have the skill, equipment or indeed finance' to
manage their own affairs. Here was a sweeping condemnation
of the whole idea without, it seemed, any effort being made to
understand what it really meant.

They decided to go for a meeting with the city engineer
himself, Mr Cuksey. And this time the Weller Streets would be
representing themselves, and would take the lead. The
engineers' response was just the latest in a long line of setbacks
where the 'professionals' had insisted on handling it themselves. This time the professionals would be there as advisers
to the co-op, who'd be expressing in person the ideals, and the
community support, they represented.

The meeting was held on 9 April in CDS's Bold Street
offices. It's not easy to disentangle the myth from the reality in
people's memories: as Bill Halsall puts it, 'Things like the
meeting with city engineers which everybody recounts: it's
become a very highly stylized version of events.' Paul Lusk
says this happened because 'You could never go back to a
meeting with a negative report, you had to go back with a
success.' But in Bill Halsall's view it wasn't just the general
membership they were trying to convince, in putting together
'a version to be reported back to the people....It was
something they had deliberately to do in order to maintain

confidence in themselves, their own faith that it would happen.'

'They' were the 'core activists' in Rory's phrase, the nucleus who met in Wilkie's before and after co-op meetings. Three of them were the Weller Streets' contingent at the engineers' meeting: Billy, Kevin and Philip. They sat down on one side of the white table in CDS's meeting room, fresh from their pre-meeting in the pub, prepared as they saw it to meet the engineers halfway: ready to propose joint maintenance of the courtyard areas.

To the co-op it was a conflict between them and the bureaucracy about the ideas behind the scheme, and behind the co-op itself. But to the professionals involved it was part of a wider debate. The co-op was, unwittingly, in the 'progressive' corner: 'In the new towns,' as Bill Halsall describes it, 'they have a development corporation where planners, architects, engineers work more as a team. So the standards that get drawn up show the influence of these other professionals... The more successful new towns' estates have narrower roads, to exclude heavy vehicles, to make it safe for children playing.'

These were the same ideas that had driven Kevin, in particular, to push the small courtyards, the landscaping, the cobbled parking areas. But against that view, as Bill puts it: 'The engineers' logic is a safe road with room to turn a lorry in, footpaths for pedestrians to walk on, gentle curves to drive safely... It also goes back to local government reorganization: where the city engineers act as the county's agents, and a certain amount of buck-passing goes on.'

The co-op saw the main issue as their credibility; the engineers as the long-standing argument with trendy planners and architects. So the city engineer himself didn't turn up. Instead, Billy recounts, 'Cuksey sent, like, two lieutenants, and they were very well briefed on it: like Tweedledum and Tweedledee.' Philip: 'The senior of the two was an elderly feller. He was just there to say "You're not getting it." So he was calm and cool. The other feller, we had the impression he was trying to make an impression on the senior feller.'

It gradually became clear that the engineers were 'well briefed' to listen and then say no. Billy: 'They had a set of rules and regulations and there was no way they were going to fucking bend them. "These rules are there for everybody's benefit..."' The co-op had carefully rehearsed all the arguments against them: to no avail. 'They had a go at the landscaping: "Do you really want the maintenance problems?" We said, "Can't we share the maintenance problems with the Council?" We proposed that: "You'll maintain the roads and the grassed areas, and we'll maintain the shrub part of it." "It won't work. We do a range of red and green tarmac, you'll be better off with that."'

The ideas weren't getting through. 'It'd been going on for about an hour and a half,' Billy says. 'We tried loads of different manoeuvres and they kept going back to these rules, how they were well thought out, well conceived.' Finally they came close to a real confrontation. Philip remembers:

'He said, "You can't turn an articulated lorry round in a courtyard." We pointed out we'd no articulated lorry drivers on the site, and a very low car ownership, and 85 per cent car spaces.' Then they came to fire hazards: a subject that had already been debated in the Inside/Outside and at general meetings. Philip recalls the younger of the engineers saying, '"The fire engine won't be able to get into the courtyards." Kevin said, "How long is the hose?" We pointed out the furthest [house] away from any access is ten to twenty yards. Kevin pointed out you had to unravel the fucking hose to get the water out. He [Kevin] said: "You know if you get a fire in Everton Towers, d'you put the fire engine in the lift and take it up to the tenth floor?"'

Kevin got angry. 'You're a fucking liar, you' – maybe he said it, maybe he didn't. But the anger was there: at all the work the co-op had put in, to be treated with contempt by bureaucrats.

And the younger of the engineers got angry too. 'The senior feller was smiling and we were smiling,' says Philip. The other man 'got his bag and he put all his stuff in his briefcase. "If that's all we're going to do, score points off each other, I'm off." As he stood the senior feller shook his head. He sat down again.' On Billy's account: 'All the fucking drawings were getting put in the briefcase. Byrnesy knocked the chair over getting up, and stood by the door, and his mate said, "Hey Arthur, calm down..."'

Yet after the anger the mood of the meeting changed for the better. The co-op's contingent were becoming resigned to the engineers' role at the meeting being, as Philip puts it, to 'just play your community politics and come back'. And in turn the older of the engineers softened. According to Billy he said, 'Why don't you have it unadopted? If you're well set-up the way you say you are, why don't you do it? If you let us in on it, you'll ruin it. Do you realize that our maintenance cycle is that a road gets repaved every ninety years?' He then got subjected to the Lancia test by Kevin: 'Byrnesy said, "Where d'you live, then?" He said, "I don't know how you know, but I live in Cheshire." I think his road was unadopted, where he lived, you know.'

At first the engineers had treated the co-op as an inferior form of public housing. Now, with the softening of mood, they began to draw comparisons with a suburban housing estate. 'That happened a lot with everything,' Billy feels. 'It was the first of its kind, so it was having to work under constraints nobody had thought out. We were treated as like the Council, or private – when we're neither.'

The co-op emerged from the meeting with nothing gained. But over discussion in the pub afterwards a vivid and positive version of events came together, to show the rest of the members they'd put up a good fight. 'It was very much a question', according to Paul Lusk, 'of the committee deciding what they dared tell the members [because] they didn't want to undermine people's hopes.' If you believed in it, though, it'd come true:

that's what the nucleus felt. They met in Wilkie's before the management committee meeting that same night to decide what 'we' would say. Philip Hughes describes how he'd originally joined this group: 'I'd go to a meeting and somebody'd say, "We thought this'd be a good idea," I decided I'd find out who "we" was. I said to Margie one night, "I'm going over to Wilkie's for a pint." I got talking to Billy and Kevin and I found out who "we" was. Yes, a lot of the thinking got done in the pub.'

The management committee heard that 'a strong case' had been put forward and that 'City engineers promised to have a look at the situation again, and would come back again with their report.'

Those at the meeting with the engineers knew in their hearts what the response would be. When it came, it was in the softer mood of the end of the meeting: 'I consider that the interest shown by the members of the cooperative in maintaining these courts to their own requirements, is such that it is preferable from their point of view, for the courts to remain private.'

Billy wrote back on behalf of the co-op to get the record straight, and perhaps to give a lingering impression of a fight not easily conceded: 'If you are still not clear about our plans, to briefly explain, our intention is to build a rural village in the heart of a dilapidated inner city area and rehabilitate a community... Mr Salter and Mr Parkes liked and completely endorsed our scheme in every respect except in their official capacity as engineers...'

There was no great enthusiasm for the idea of the co-op doing its own maintenance. In Billy's recollection, 'The only definite decision was, "Look they're not going to give way here so we'll just proceed and hope the standards change." There wasn't anything like, "Let's go ahead with it unadopted."'*

---

*Ironically the city engineers did later relax their standards on adoption, but too late to help the Weller Streets.

The Inside/Outside were now trying to prepare for the next stage of the design, the application to the Housing Corporation and the Department of the Environment (DoE) for 'cost yardstick' approval: the approval of the design of the scheme, and the setting of a cost limit for it. They invited two people from the DoE down to see them. Charlie Barnes, the Regional Architect, arrived, accompanied by Bill Halsall. After the introductory formalities the co-op people told Bill Halsall to leave so they could discuss things directly. 'You've scored points for that, lad,' said Charlie Barnes. It soon emerged that he'd been brought up in a terraced house like the Weller Streets. Amid shared memories of sleeping in a bedroom divided by a blanket hung on a washing line, his sympathy for the co-op rapidly became clear, as the management committee minutes record:

> Mr Barnes was most impressed by the Weller Sts Co-op and appreciated all the effort put in to make the scheme work. Mr Barnes advised Weller Sts not to become bureaucrats and to take legal advice. Mr Barnes promised to do everything possible for the Weller Sts in the way of AD HOCS. K Byrne felt that the visit was a great success for both parties.

Preparation for the 'cost yardstick' application involved the quantity surveyor, Gordon Tait of local firm Houghton and Stackpoole. His firm had been appointed to the project back in June 1978; the co-op had simply endorsed the recommendation of CDS and BDG. 'Unlike the architects,' Martine had written to the co-op at the time, 'quantity surveyors stay in the background, merely keeping a close watch on the costs.'

Gordon now stepped into the foreground to talk to the Inside/Outside about 'inadmissible costs': the costs of items which the co-op might have to find ways of paying for itself, because they were above government standards. Unfortunately that wasn't how he explained it. Billy and one or two others had had their usual pint before a meeting. Gordon started off talking in jargon. Kitty was there: 'Gordon only said a few words and Billy said, "Fuck off, I don't understand a word you're saying."' As Gordon himself puts it, with characteristic mildness, 'There was a complaint in quite forceful terms. It's not easy, after spending your lifetime talking in technical terms, to bring this down into terms which people can readily understand.'

'Down' is maybe a key word here. Rozzie Lybert was a general member who'd been persuaded along to this meeting. She says it was 'like they were talking down to us. They were discussing things with themselves, talking way above us.' Not everybody approved of the way Billy dealt with it. Kitty says she and Irene 'didn't like Billy saying that, 'cause it made little of someone in front of us, and we wouldn't have liked it if it was done to us'. But the point got home: Gordon himself reflected on it, and accepted it.

The general membership didn't even know who Gordon Tait was. They didn't much care, perhaps, where the design was up to. They wanted to know if the co-op was really going to get the land.

At last, over March and April, CDS and the solicitors had managed to sort out the legal problems over buying the site: though not before, at one meeting, 'CDS apologized for their handling of the matter.' The site was to become the co-op's on 11 May: it was decided to have a celebration on the following Sunday, the 13th.

Fund-raising and co-op dos had been held erratically since the co-op began. The 'paper chase' and rag collections had long since died the death. Steve Cossack had organized a few dances in aid of the co-op, but it was all a bit of a hotch-potch. The committee decided they should really put some effort into the celebrations this time. Kate Kelly's interest was stirred. She thought the co-op was more of a realistic idea, if they really were getting the site. And she and her daughter Kitty had always been known for organizing parties in the streets. Kate says, 'Kitty proposed, "Why don't we have a walkabout carnival?"'

Kitty's idea was to have a Dickensian theme, to go with the names of the streets. 'We decided', she says, 'we'd walk down from the Weller Streets to the land. We wanted everybody in the area to know this was ours.' While men dominated the committee of the co-op, women were in the majority at meetings. One man, Sammy Roberts, echoes the view of many in saying he thought women 'spread the word better. They talk their own language which we [men] never. They were on what you'd call a ghost committee; through verbal talking or meeting on Park Road.'

The 'ghost committee' had done a lot of the foot-slogging: from the early days of getting people interested to going around with the petitions for the partnership application, as Ivy Stead recounts, 'We walked the Holy Land for signatures for a community centre.' Now the ghost committee got to work on the carnival preparations. 'It was put together with nothing,' says Billy Floyd. 'Not a lot of expense, just an awful lot of fucking effort.' There were Kitty and Kate, Ivy and Irene, Ann Byrne and Thelma Floyd, Ethel Barwise and Alice White, and many more. They ran up Dickensian costumes; prepared food; got a good supply of drink in.

That Sunday turned out to be the warmest, sunniest day of the entire spring. Crowds came out to see the parade. Kitty: 'I can still remember a lady coming out of one of the houses over there [overlooking the site] with two big trifles and saying, "Here, love, add this to your party."' Ivy Stead remembers: 'Billy Floyd and Thelma were dressed up as Mr and Mrs Micawber. Kate and Kitty and all of them, they were matchbox men and all kinds of sweets. They marched all round the area with the Fou Fou band, then they marched down here [to the site]. There were games and ale and that.'

One of the games was to pelt Steve Cossack with wet sponges while he stood in the stocks. It was meant for the kids but a few adults couldn't resist having a go too. There was a 'dig-in' too: to dig up stone setts from the site to be used later in the landscaping. Ivy Stead: 'It was going on for two years before it was really off the ground. When they come and told us they'd got the money, we had the carnival and then the dig-in.'

For people to whom the two years up to now had merely seemed 'dreaming', the carnival, the buying of the site made it seem more real. The next day their names were in the papers: 'PICKWICK CAPERS' said the *Daily Mail*, with pictures of the children dressed up. Perhaps not surprisingly, the *Mail* didn't feature what had been written on a wall still standing on the site. Billy: 'The slogan we put on the wall was thought up on the spur of the moment: "THIS LAND NOW BELONGS TO THE PEOPLE". So we said, "Who can paint?" Georgie Smith. So he painted it. That was the first time a lot of people felt: Fucking hell, it's going to work, this.'

'It became more interesting after they acquired the site,' says Rozzie Lybert. 'Before, it was all on paper: a fantasy.' Her cousin Billy felt the same: 'They had a parade. From that point on I believed in it.'

But the actual houses were still only paper houses; still a fantasy. A few weeks after the carnival the wall – complete with its proud slogan, 'THIS LAND NOW BELONGS TO THE PEOPLE' – fell down. There was still a long way to go.

6

Burning the Boats:
The Bureaucrats Say Yes

The co-op had existed for nearly two years. At last they owned their own land. The intense work committee members had put in was beginning to pay off.

Yet some of the general membership showed as little interest now as they had in the beginning. Harry Dono: 'A lot of people, you'd say to them, "We're going to form a co-op." And they'd say, "Agh, heard it all before…" In other words, *you* can put in as many hours as you like, shite on *your* social life.' The committee could only go so far in encouraging general members: they had to show some commitment too. The minimum they had to do was to attend one general meeting – held roughly monthly – in three. As Harry says, you spend as long waiting for a bus over that sort of period. People were supposed to give a reason if they didn't come to a meeting, but that hadn't made any difference while people thought nothing would happen.

The committee decided to crack down. Billy Floyd thinks, 'We must have said, "Look, the pace is hotting up, it's getting really different, this game, we can't carry passengers."' As Philip recalls Billy's line at the time: 'We've no fucking passengers. We're not fucking BEA.'

They were careful to be fair; they had to be. 'No one ever set their stall out to get anybody,' Peter Tyrrell says. 'We'd get the membership register and if people had missed three meetings they were recommended for expulsion. Everyone who was proposed for expulsion always had the right to go to the meeting. We always gave them the right to go to the management committee too.'

Those recommended for expulsion – five in the first instance – were given twenty-eight days' notice of the intention to expel them at a special general meeting to be called for the purpose. Philip Hughes remembers: 'We had five people that all went on at the same time. We gave them twenty-eight days. Three of them didn't reply. Two came. It was pretty unsavoury, y'know. We said, "Why haven't you been in contact?" This one turned round and said, "I'm telling nobody my fucking business."'

'What it went back to all the time,' Philip says, 'was we knew each other, we lived in each other's pockets.' Some would say, 'I'm on my own with the children.' But children were never excluded from meetings; some brought them along if they couldn't fix a sitter. Some would say, 'I'm on shifts.' But Steve Cossack and Billy Odger were too.

Rumours went round about what the committee were doing. Lily Faulkner remembers: 'Another rumour went round. This person in North Hill Street: "Living with that crowd," he said, "I believe if you have a row with your neighbour you get evicted. You're all a big clique," he said.' Sammy Roberts: 'Sometimes you'd get pulled up in the pub: "Who d'you think youse are? You can't tell people who're going to get houses or not. Who are you?"'

Against this background it was vital to play it dead straight. One of the first five to be recommended for expulsion was a relative of Kitty's. It showed no favour was being given. The committee presented it in the hardest way they'd presented anything to a general meeting (the minutes are recorded in block capitals, as if to emphasize the seriousness of the issue):

THE METHOD OF DISMISSAL IS BY VOTING. THE MEMBERSHIP VOTE EITHER FOR OR AGAINST THE

COMMITTEE'S DECISION, AND A 2/3 MAJORITY IS
NEEDED TO CARRY THAT DECISION. THE CHAIR-
MAN STATED, HOWEVER, THAT IF THE VOTE GOES
AGAINST THE COMMITTEE, THE COMMITTEE WILL
TAKE IT AS A VOTE OF NO CONFIDENCE AND WILL
STAND DOWN AND A NEW COMMITTEE WILL HAVE
TO BE ELECTED.

At that meeting, on 4 June 1979, there were forty-two votes
for the expulsions; two against; no abstentions. Sammy, a
moderate on many issues, was hard-line on this one. 'We had
to do these things once they started wavering. If you're not
going to fight for them, you want to be off. That's why it was
so solid.' He emphasizes, as many do, the emotions people felt
behind the ruthlessness. 'Bear in mind it was heart-breaking at
times, it was heart-breaking telling them they weren't on,
when they realized. We told 'em straight, "Here you are, voice
your opinion." Then "All in favour" and they were out
... Sometimes you'd bring it home to the wife and say, "We
had to expel her," and she'd say, "Oh, that's hard."'

Peter Tyrrell adds, though, 'I never felt any remorse or
anything. The only sadness I felt was the lost opportunity. I
think they thought the committee was a lot of fucking
dickheads and they could just swan around week after week
and get their house at the end.'

To replace the people expelled, and those who'd left the area
and resigned, the co-op had a waiting list. At this time you had
to live in the Weller Streets area to be on the list. Then, when
vacancies arose, your membership record was checked and
people spoke about what contribution you'd made to the co-
op. Ivy Stead: 'It went according to who attended the meetings
the most, whether you'd bought raffle tickets and that.'
Sammy feels that, too, made for greater solidarity. 'Some
weakened and dropped out. The more dropped out, the
stronger we got really: 'cause the ones that were left were
fighting.'

But the main 'fighters' were still the committee. Most of them had been on more or less from the beginning: Billy and Kevin, Kitty and Irene, Harry Dono and Bill Odger, the Robertses, Peter Tyrrell. Two people's involvement began to fade around this time: Eifion Wynn-Jones resigned as treasurer: he had family problems, and then got a job away from Liverpool. And Steve Cossack resigned from the committee for personal reasons.

Stephen Rice was still the 'education' specialist, and was also the co-op's representative on the CDS management committee: the nature of his work with the co-op brought him into closer contact with CDS than the others, and he enjoyed the committee work despite his avowed dislike of committees. Dickie Sharp, the retired docker, had taken over as Minutes Secretary, and was also persuaded to take over the books when Eifion resigned: he was a fastidious and well-liked man. And Philip Hughes, who'd been the Vice-Chairman, became 'Acting Secretary'. Philip remembers Billy labelling him as the 'pedant'. He'd always been a union man: 'There was a couple of times I've almost become a steward: but the steward I've always had has been good.' Philip was the man behind the steward, the man pushing the Chairman: coming over sometimes as a bit stroppy, a bit aggressive, always asking the awkward question. 'Excuse me, you're acting incorrectly there,' Billy says he'd say.

Philip it was who at the end of May brought up a ticklish issue at the management committee:

P. Hughes thinks it would be unfair for members to move out of area, then move back into Miles Byles and make capital out of the Co-op. He would like a redraft of the rules. Houses are for need not for greed. W. Floyd agreed he was morally right but it would be hard to impose a redraft of the rules.

It wasn't just that people were moving out of the area; they were buying their own houses, but retaining a share in the co-op. Ann Caddis was one: 'We moved into Dingle Lane 'cause we were overcrowded. We had two boys in the one room and a girl in our room. It was mentioned at the meeting about people moving house. But Steve Cossack had already done it, he'd moved to Vining Street.' Arthur Roberts bought his own house a little later too; and Kitty Heague had been rehoused by CDS because of her overcrowding. 'There was a lot of comment about it,' as Billy Floyd recalls, ''cause it was only the ones on the committee that seemed to be doing it.'

As one member puts it: 'If you're on the committee, you should be irreproachable.' Billy as chairman was in a dilemma. Personally he felt: 'I think it was the duty of those who were still in there to nail their colours to the mast and stick in there.' On the other hand, some people had already done it. And they'd done it to relieve their housing conditions, which was after all the objective of the co-op. Billy: 'Could we say, "How dare you get yourself a bathroom and an inside toilet while we're fighting the war?"'

No one ever forced the issue: by default, it was permitted. As usual when an awkward issue arose, it had fallen on Billy to try and sort it out. He felt most pressure, but all of the committee were feeling it by June 1979: from outside organizations, from members, from families. Sammy Roberts says: 'We were all getting told off by our wives: "You might as well live in the bloody co-op." We'd go to the pub and we'd come out singing and dancing. We had to face it both ways. If we never went to the meetings, we'd get told off. If we went, when we came back we'd get told off.'

The committee had been trying since June 1978 to get a grant from the Housing Corporation for their own paid worker to take some of the burden off them. But the money only finally came through in June 1979, and was for an 'education' worker: more because that was the only way you could get a grant, than because that was what Weller Streets wanted. No one in the co-op had experience of employing people. But because they wanted their worker to be independent, they were a bit wary of CDS's advice on the subject.

The result was a long and detailed job description that no one person would ever have been able to do, and an over-large interviewing panel. Sue Jackson – no longer with CDS – was one of the candidates. 'I had the feeling,' she recalls, 'that they wanted somebody they could control. They didn't actually want somebody who was going to tell them what to do.'

Joe Corbett got the job. Like the inner group of the management committee he was in his twenties, had just started a family, and was of socialist sympathies. Not from Liverpool, he'd been on the fringes of community work in Liverpool for a few years. He knew Rory Heap; through Rory he'd made contact with the Weller Streets in late 1977 and had written a couple of articles about them for a community newspaper, the *Liverpool 8 Express*. In 1978 he'd worked for the Toxteth Community Council – for a day – before the grant for his job got cut off.

He began work on 31 July 1979. 'It was as much a learning process for me as for them,' he says. The start of his employment was uneasy. 'It became apparent that they didn't know what they wanted. I expected more active support than there was when I got there. I felt very isolated from the people. I had a number of discussions with Billy and Stephen Rice, and also Bill went to see Rory, 'cause I think he was getting a lot of flak from people.'

As usual, the onus was on Billy to sort it out. 'He didn't qualify for his money,' Billy remembers people saying to him. 'Early days before Joe, I did most of the writing, or Rory and I did it together. Then Joe arrived and they couldn't see...' People couldn't see, if Joe was simply relieving people like Billy or Stephen Rice or Dickie Sharp of work, what he was contributing. And, as Peter Tyrrell says, 'He took the brunt of a lot of stuff he shouldn't have really got blamed for. 'Cause it was decided in committee, people decided it was Joe's job to do it.'

Joe also looked and acted like a student. 'I said to Joe,' Billy remembers, 'these people work in schedules. You need to get up at nine o'clock and show them you're working.' With inexperience of employment on both sides, and Billy with some help from Stephen Rice left to sort it out in amongst all the other co-op business, it took a long time to settle down. 'I had to learn about the co-op very quickly,' Joe recalls, 'what its aims were, the way it approached things.'

In June the co-op finally got its own office: a terraced house in the area, 16 Pecksniff Street, licensed from CDS. And in September/October a new range of sub-committees were established: fund-raising, education/information and building. Joe feels that helped to clarify the work-load. 'It was resolved by both sides realizing we hadn't been having a focus. It picked up after that as the demand of the work escalated. I was establishing the office – their enormous quantity of records; trying to get them into some sort of system...servicing the management committee and the sub-committees.'

But even then difficulties remained. As the minutes of a management committee in November, when Joe was on leave, say:

> It was generally agreed that a working formula be worked out for Joe Corbett. In order for more service to be given to Gen/Man Committee and Sub committees and collection on Monday nights. There was a feeling for a speeding up on membership contacts and news sheets.

Joe and the others recognized his strength: 'I seemed to be able to put down things on paper in a way that would get across to people who weren't picking up paper every day of the week.' But Joe wasn't the kind of man they were used to dealing with. Peter: 'You couldn't challenge Joe very heavily 'cause he'd just break down...and I couldn't handle that.' Billy Floyd became friendly with Joe through their working partnership, but it frustrated him too: 'I had a very clear idea what I wanted from him, and he never fucking did it.'

Inevitably, though, the employment of a worker was going to have its complications as well as relieving some of the pressure. The demands on the committee were mounting. Joe took over the minutes from Dickie Sharp so he could concentrate on the treasurer's job (though in practice Dickie's job was wider than that). Joe set up the office. And with Stephen Rice he began, in October 1979, to put more work into the revamped 'Education' committee.

Stephen had already, in the spring of that year, begun to get the general membership involved in a 'Rules for All' game with the idea of getting the basis for the future tenancy agreement out of it. Rob Macdonald, working closely with the co-op up to March 1979, had thought of the 'Education' committee: 'I felt they were on the outside. That's an interesting thing, how effective it was; and if they were able to educate themselves without having to go through established routines.'

Part of that sense of them being 'on the outside' stemmed from Stephen's way of working. 'Stephen Rice, he wasn't as close as the other men,' Kitty says. 'He was like the go-between on the committee: Education and Information Officer: so he had more dealings with CDS.' And indeed, as Rob suggests, some of the 'education' the committee had gone through had been outside established routines: through working with Rory Heap, they'd learnt to practise for meetings, and to try and work things out for themselves; through Bill Halsall they'd developed skills in designing.

But Stephen's particular preoccupation was the 'education' not just of committee members, but of the general membership too. The 'Rules for All' game was something he'd picked up from Tony Gibson, an academic from Nottingham, who was interested in community action and adult education based on the community; and who was interested in using packs and games to help people learn.

Tony Gibson hadn't endeared himself to a group of the men early on. A few of them had turned out one Sunday morning in the Labour rooms in Admiral Street, to try out one of his 'education packs' and be video'd doing it. The game involved putting together a cardboard house and fitting the furniture into it. Bill Halsall was there as an observer too: 'It lasted about half an hour. There was all this messing around with the camera. Phil and Kevin started...' They started trying to take it moderately seriously, but 'it became apparent that the scale was all to cock.'

The session degenerated. They described for the benefit of the video how they were now putting an 8-foot high cooker in a 7-foot-6-inches high room. They pretended the cardboard figures were people in the co-op; for the video they described how a woman was standing on the toilet seat to see if her husband was coming home pissed. 'What I remember was,' Bill Halsall says, 'Phil started to tell him all about tolerances, how important it was in reducing scale to keep the tolerances right.' Philip knew about these problems from his work. In the end, Philip recalls, 'Floydie said, "They're open, boys. Put his coat on; and we're all off."'

The men on the committee didn't like 'playing at it'. Some of them felt the same about the 'Rules for All' exercise. This involved turning over cards: a different colour depending on whether you said yes, no or don't know to a question (e.g. 'Should people be allowed to keep dogs?') The cards told you the rule you'd come up with. Kevin in particular hated it. Philip went along with it, although he was dubious: 'It wasn't the straight way of making decisions, the sort of union way of making decisions...From the outset: who writes out the fucking cards?'

But first Stephen, and then Stephen and Joe together with help from Dickie, got small groups of the members in to play the game. And among the wider membership the game was popular. 'They were a bit tickled by it,' Billy Floyd says, 'especially the older ones. It looked the part. We're not all sitting, teacher–pupil stuff.' And Billy feels it made an important contribution: 'Stephen's one of those people, unlike the rest of us, who's really impressed by the professionals. It did work: it was the foundation for the tenancy agreements. He worked a long time over that, Ricey.' Stephen's zeal for it, though, back-fired on him a bit with the rest of the committee. 'He went on about it that much that he took some ridicule from Philip and that. [But] if we hadn't've done that, we'd have had a lot of wrangling.'

The game helped to involve the general membership. And it began to prepare the co-op for the eventual management of the scheme. At the same time, in the autumn of 1979, the co-op was beginning to feel apprehensive about that. They had a few sessions from the CDS Housing Manager (myself) about what the management would involve. They began to talk about the implications of the courts for how they might manage themselves: in small groups, or as a whole? And they started to think about whether they needed an agency like CDS in the long run, or whether they could manage on their own.

The general membership was also drawn in more by the growing fund-raising activities in 1979. The success of the carnival had shown what the 'ghost committee' of women could do; and the acquisition of their own office and worker meant that more funds were needed. So after Steve Cossack resigned from the committee, Kitty, Irene, Ann Byrne and Thelma Floyd got together to form the fund-raising committee. They quickly drew in some of the older women too: Kate, Ethel Barwise, Ivy Stead, Alice White. Kate says: 'I could never go to the early meetings 'cause I used to stay and mind her kids. Then she [Kitty] said they were forming a fund-raising committee, would I like to be on it?' They started off with a rummage sale, and with properly organizing the 10p subs people were supposed to pay each week. Then they started up coffee afternoons. Kate: 'When we got the fund-raising we started trying to do something weekly or fortnightly to keep everyone together: and it worked.' They'd meet in the office, and play bingo, and get talking. Kitty says, 'They're discussing the co-op as well; they're learning, where they won't ask at the meeting.' The momentum built up, Kate remembers: 'After we started the coffee afternoons and they were a success – then somebody said we'll have a drink: so we had the cheese and wine.'

The third sub-committee that got working in September/October was the Building Committee. The Inside/Outside's work had been more or less completed by May, and it had fizzled out. In June Martine of CDS had gathered together and sent off the 'yardstick' application: with drawings from Bill Halsall, costs from Gordon Tait, and a short history of the co-op written by Paul Lusk. Progress on the design needed to wait till the bureaucrats at the Housing Corporation and the DoE had considered the co-op's proposals. The application had had to begin at the beginning again, explaining what the co-op was about:

> The scheme is unique for two main reasons: Firstly, the control by the Co-operative over the design process from inception, is a radically new development in the field of co-operative housing.... Secondly, the Co-operative's design philosophy itself questions and challenges traditional approaches to new-build housing.... Finally, these sketch scheme proposals are made by people who currently live in rapidly deteriorating clearance housing. These circumstances command a swift appraisal of the submission...

All this was all very well, this 'radical' and 'challenge' and 'command'; but administratively the co-op's scheme was a scheme like any other. It had to wait its turn in the paperwork queue. Besides, from the Housing Corporation's point of view, it came through those stroppy CDS people. And it was cluttered with other issues they were raising: extra fees for the architect to cover the 'educational' element of the work they'd done; and a request for permission to employ a landscape architect in view of the crucial importance of the landscaping to the design.

Nothing seemed to happen for a couple of months. CDS took some flak for this. Joe Corbett wrote to Catherine Meredith in August saying, 'There is a feeling that progress has been somewhat erratic of late.' But CDS had been doing their best. They'd been in – in bureaucratic terms, heated – correspondence over the architects' fees and the need for a landscape architect. They kept chasing up the Housing Corporation.

But for the committee that wasn't good enough. Catherine Meredith hadn't kept to her undertaking to come to the management committee fortnightly; both Paul and Martine had been on leave at the same time; and memories of earlier dealings made them suspicious. Joe Corbett recalls: 'Rather than panic about it, I think Billy said, "Well, OK, we'll ...stand or fall by it, not CDS. So we'll adopt a direct negotiating position."' They fixed a meeting with the Housing Corporation and the DoE without CDS representation.

Just before the meeting a special Council sub-committee had given the co-op's scheme planning permission, subject to the co-op covenanting to maintain the non-adopted areas. The committee's early contacts with planning officers and politicians had paid off. Armed with this official endorsement of their ideas, the co-op prepared to tackle the meeting aggressively, hopeful of support from Charlie Barnes, the DoE architect who'd shown such interest in their ideas when he'd visited them in May.

The meeting was held on 19 September in the Housing Corporation's offices in town. 'The meeting began', recalls Max Steinberg of the Housing Corporation, 'in a very strange way when Billy Floyd, I think it was, announced that he was going to chair the meeting....Once he'd made an initial statement we then got down to discussing the matters at issue.'

The co-op representatives – Billy, Kevin and Dickie – with Joe there to take the co-op's own minutes of the meeting – queried the fact that the local boss of the Housing Corporation, Mike Clarke, wasn't at the meeting. The Housing Corporation people assured them they had delegated power; and in turn queried why CDS weren't there.

The meeting didn't go the co-op's way. While Charlie Barnes of the DoE was sympathetic to the co-op, he was careful to operate strictly within the administrative rules. He made his impartiality clear when he 'wiped the floor with Halsall', as Billy recalls. '"What've you done it on this grid for, lad?" We're all sitting there, thinking, "This is a good start, this."' The plans had been submitted on the wrong scale. Although the meeting was held nearly three months after the original application, the official minutes record: 'Due to every effort having been made, the scheme had been processed more quickly than usual. DoE agreed with this statement. Weller Streets accepted this.'

Throughout the meeting, Max recalls, Billy 'continued to regard himself as Chairman. But nevertheless we got through all the points that we wanted to get through.' Higher architects' fees? – No. A landscape architect? – No. Higher standards like more insulation than the minimum government standard? – No, but try applying to a charitable trust.

It's a meeting many people remember – the 'tripartite meeting' – even though relatively little happened at it. Perhaps it was because it was the first time the co-op hadn't had CDS beside them at an important meeting: they did it on their own. Perhaps it was because it was the first time they'd met formally with the bureaucrats who were to loan them the money for the scheme.

And, as Max Steinberg himself says, 'I can see, looking back, it was one of those times when the scheme stood in the balance.' What *wasn't* said was as important as what *was* said. Nobody queried the basic idea of the design. Nobody queried the way the design had been done. Nobody, after the initial doubt about why CDS weren't there, questioned the right of the Weller Streets to be there, talking as equals with government officials.

It was also the beginning of something. 'From that point on,' Joe Corbett says, 'there was all the trips down to Fenwick Street without appointments...' The Weller Streets began to hound the life out of Max Steinberg at the Housing Corporation, though it still took till February 1980 for the approval to come through. They'd tend to stroll into Max's office after a quick pint and ask him what was happening. Billy says, 'I understood the constraints he was under. He was never obnoxious. We did take occasional liberties with him. I think he did always try and understand: "Shit, they're trying to get out of that fucking mess."'

Max himself became quite accustomed to their approach. 'They were keen to progress their scheme. And I think as a result of their anxiety to ensure that nothing stood in their way, they tended to try and use aggression as an initial tactic – to bulldoze their way through what they saw as red tape or bureaucracy. Having said that, they undoubtedly had a sense of humour; and, when you sat down with them, a sense of reality.'

So Max became, like Charlie Barnes, a bureaucrat who felt sympathy with them, 'a sense they were doing something worthwhile sharing in', within the administrative rules. But it all took time. By the autumn of 1979 time was becoming a vital factor. Conditions were beginning to deteriorate badly in the area. The public inquiry into the clearance order had been held in July 1979; official confirmation of it seemed imminent. CDS houses weren't being re-let; boarded up houses began to dot the streets.

Billy Odger recalls, 'I think a lot dropped off during it, 'cause it was taking too long. We tried to explain it wasn't us, it was just the government red tape to get the money.' This was the pressure at the committee's backs while the bureaucrats were explaining to them the inevitable delays. It became doubly important to bind the general membership in to the idea, through the fund-raising, and the 'Rules for All' game, and regular general meetings, as conditions in the streets worsened.

The committee organized the allocations: who'd get what house or flat. Originally it had been Martine's idea to use the answer to the questionnaire question about who wanted to live next to whom as the basis for who got what. But the committee decided that would be too complicated. And, against the perennial need to show fairness, without favour, a committee decision of any kind would be open to attack.

Instead they drew numbers out of a hat. Over a number of general meetings – to help keep up interest – a group of people picked by lot their house or flat. If they wanted to live somewhere in particular, or in a particular spot, they had to agree an exchange with someone else. Lily Durrant and Ada Hewitt, for instance, were two elderly sisters who wanted to be in flats next door to each other (there were to be two flats at the corner of each courtyard). As Lily describes it: 'To save anyone saying, "She's got the best flat," they said, "How about getting a number and drawing it out of a hat"... I had the top flat over there and I said to Kitty, "We'd have liked to have got together." So – I've forgot her name – so we swapped.'

In amongst this drive to get and keep the general members involved, there was a sudden and unexpected setback. The new building committee had begun in October to talk with Bill Halsall and Dave Wilkinson, the other partner in BDG, about the detailed design for the 'working drawings' that would soon need to be done. The programme agreed by everyone up to now had shown building starting on site in 1980. In November 1979 Dave Wilkinson told them it couldn't be done. Joe Corbett recalls: 'The... issue then was, when could the earliest start on site take place? There was a lot of disagreement between Dave Wilkinson and the co-op. Dave was of the view, he gave February 1981 as the earliest projected date, which clearly for the co-op was far too late. Billy was concerned, there were so many years of campaigning and not even a bit of chicken wire fence to show for it.'

Martine of CDS was a frequent attender of meetings at this time. She took up cudgels on behalf of the co-op. In writing to BDG she said: 'Let me stress that the Professional Advisers are the very last quarters from where the Co-operative should expect an undermining of the scheme success...'

That way of putting it offended people in BDG. They'd still received no fees for their work, but Bill Halsall in particular had put an enormous amount of time and effort into it. Nevertheless they did agree to speed up the work. Bill Halsall and a technician, and Gordon Tait the quantity surveyor would go ahead at risk on preparing for tenders, despite the lack of any formal official approval.

The pressure caused by the deteriorating conditions also showed in the departure from the co-op in December 1979 of Harry Dono, the first of the original committee members to leave. He and his wife Liz had bought their own house on an outlying estate. Liz had been the victim of a particularly frightening burglary the previous January, and wanted out.

To some of the men on the committee this was an example of 'wife trouble'. Sue Jackson says, 'I remember from talking to Martine there were a lot of other wives who made that stand: pressure on husbands to spend less time on co-op affairs: what she called "wife trouble".' But it was very hard for people like Liz Dono, Cathy Cossack, Ada Odger and the other wives of committee members, often left alone in the house while their husbands went to meetings and then on to the the the pub. Liz herself says: 'I found many a time I didn't understand what was going on. I'd say, "Have you got any further?"' After the burglary it was small wonder Liz wanted them to move. Harry himself says, 'First and foremost is the length of time it was taking. It wasn't so much the waiting, but especially after we got robbed that time, I was thinking I was going to be the last in this whole bloody block of houses.'

When the time came to resign Liz nevertheless found it hard: 'That last meeting: I took that letter over, saying we were getting our own house. As much as I was overjoyed we were getting our own house I had a lump in my throat, I didn't want to hand over that letter.'

Harry and Liz didn't think it would be right to keep their share if they moved out. There had, anyway, been other background reasons for Harry's departure. Harry felt unhappy with some of the ideas about individual choice that were being bandied about: particularly with the idea you should move if your family size changed, and that your personal choice in how to change/improve your house should be limited. He says, 'I would have been allocated a four-bedroomed house. Then one of them grew up, they'd want us to move to a three-bedroomed, then a two-bedroomed.' These are ideas Kevin, Billy, Philip and Peter would talk about: they've never been adopted as co-op policy. But the crucial thing about choice for Harry was: 'They also said, you could not alter the internal structure of the house. I said, "You can't build a brick fireplace?" And he said, "You can't"... I didn't understand that: if you move into Corporation property you've got to leave it as you found it. If the person moved in wanted it, you'd leave it. What are you saying? "You're gonna live in a barracks and y'all have the same picture over the fireplace"?'

This was the egalitarian idea Kevin had always pushed and been supported on: that everyone should have the same. In his view, what Harry wanted, 'It was people putting their own personal ideas before a co-op idea. We all lived in slums and bad housing conditions: we were all moving from that to a new fucking place.... People wanted to put their own personal choice before the community's choice.' But the issue wasn't widely debated in the 'community' at the time; Harry himself didn't raise it. Nevertheless, it was a change from the days when the committee had been proclaiming that the difference between the Weller Streets and the Corporation was the choice you got; this was an example where you'd get less choice.

So Harry and Liz left. And the pressure that had caused them to leave continued. In February 1980 the clearance order was confirmed. The Housing Department sent round a letter saying they'd be visiting shortly to talk about rehousing. How should the co-op respond? Billy Odger for one was uncertain about which way to fall. 'It was taking so long and there was so much red tape. There was the girl, sixteen, the girl, fifteen, and the lad all sleeping in one room. My wife was on to me all the time.'

But in addition, Billy Odger was also worried about the way the debate about personal choice was going. Billy Floyd recalls, before the land had even been bought, 'Odger came to our house – Luskie was having dinner – and saying, "Look, will we be able to have a green bathroom suite?" There was a fucking mountain to climb and this guy wanted a green bathroom suite.'

This was the sort of choice you got in an improvement 'co-op': a little extra you could pay for yourself. Billy Odger always wanted it. But on 5 February 1980, the Building Committee decided: 'Extras were possible providing the choices available did not incur extra costs. For example, it would be possible to have a limited choice of colours for the kitchen units, though not for bathroom suites...'

As Kevin recalls it, 'We said, "No, all the baths 'll be white." Billy Odger wanted to put down an extra thirty pounds for a turquoise bathroom suite. We said, "Can you pay for everybody to have it? What about the pensioner who can't afford it?"'

In February the Housing Department began to knock on doors to talk about rehousing. Billy Odger was among the few members who didn't say they were in the co-operative. This was unsatisfactory for the Housing Department: they wanted to know who they'd have to rehouse. It was hotly debated in the committee. 'We decided', says Philip Hughes, 'we can't do it that way...We felt there were people wanted to ride two horses in the same race.'

'STAND UP AND BE COUNTED!' said the newsletter heralding the Special General Meeting of 18 February to discuss the issue. The committee invited the local housing manager along to the meeting. Philip recalls: 'Billy got McAuliffe there and [said], "We want you to explain they've got two choices, they can either stay with us or go to the Corpie."'

That fitted in with what Mr McAuliffe wanted to say anyway. Billy Floyd began by outlining the committee's position:

> the Co-operative had agreed to liaise with the local authority, and had supplied them with the names and addresses of all the shareholders. Given that approval had been granted to go ahead with the development of the Miles/Byles Street site, and given that the housing would be purpose-built in accordance with the wishes and needs of the membership, it was curious that some members had apparently denied to the local authority that they were shareholders.

Then Mr McAuliffe spoke for the Housing Department. As Irene recalls: 'He told us the kind of place they could give us: Netherley, Kirkby, Speke. I think it was him said one in forty or one in thirty would get somewhere local. He gave us the figures for new-build: they'd only built fifty or sixty houses in the past seven years.'

In some ways this was simply restating what had given rise to the co-op in the first place: the lack of decent local rehousing (except for some possible nominations to housing association houses). But it needed restating now, with the houses deteriorating, and the prospect of people not in the co-op getting rehoused before co-op members. As Philip remembers it: 'He finished off by saying, "I'm not not very proud of these facts." He said to us privately, "You're getting rehoused, aren't you?" We said, "Yes, it's a credibility gap." He said, "You've got a wonderful scheme here, I can't understand why you'd want to leave; but if you do, tell me."'

Nobody said anything at the time. But a few days after the meeting George Millington and Billy Odger, both members of the co-op from the beginning, resigned. Billy Floyd had said at the general meeting, 'if anyone wanted to take their chances with the Corporation, they were free to do so, on condition that they tendered their resignation from the Co-operative.'

Billy and Ada Odger took their chances with the Corporation at the time, though, in the event, they actually bought their own house. Other people found it hard to understand their departure. Peter Tyrrell groups them with the Donos: 'Odger and Dono... They'd both earned to get one of these. You've got to feel a great deal of sympathy for them 'cause they did work hard. I think Dono went out 'cause of the fireplace and Odger went out 'cause he couldn't have a green bath. They will always remain things I can never understand.'

The prime reason for both of them going was the pressure of circumstances and conditions. They'd both been in it from the beginning, but with less of the idea of a 'fight' than Billy, Peter, Kevin and Philip. Their motivation was more to do with their housing conditions. They were both more interested in individual choice than the others: the houses weren't going to be 'purpose-built' enough, or on site soon enough for them. As it turned out, they could both afford to buy their own houses.

It remained an uncomfortable truth, though, that there were four members who'd already moved out, three to buy their own houses, who still did 'ride two horses in the same race'. But the rest of the membership 'burnt their boats'.

They agreed to go to the bottom of the Corpie queue, on a promise from the committee that houses would be on site by the end of the year. The 'yardstick approval' came through in February: the co-op's professionals were almost set to go out to tender. Could the committee deliver on their promises?

7

The Darkest Hour:
(Not) Getting a Builder

Gordon Tait and Bill Halsall were the two professionals the committee were relying on, to help deliver the goods. By March 1980 Bill had been closely involved with the co-op for two years. Everybody knew who he was, and how involved he was. For himself, 'I realized what they expected of me was to build this dream; to give physical form to this dream and convey it to the members – a case of holding this vision there of what it was going to be like; keeping the strength of that there long enough to be able to build it.' He felt excited and fearful as the prospect of the co-op getting a builder came closer: 'I sometimes felt the responsibilities very heavily about having to deliver the goods. Being able to deliver the goods was the real test.'

Gordon Tait, as the quantity surveyor, had stayed more in the background. His relationship with the co-op had developed badly at first, with the row in April 1979 over the language he used. Billy Floyd says, 'He was all hoity-toity: "I'll have a horf of bitter." He got infected too, like.' Infection meant accepting the co-op's views of the language he used, and getting involved in the co-op himself so that he'd come to feel, he says, 'very sympathetic to their needs, and enthusiastic about the concept of co-operative housing: to counter the state of apathy that existed in public sector housing. They were very forceful people, of course, and you get swept along with them.' Normally working with other professionals, Gordon felt his attitude to his job changing through working with the Weller Streets. 'I was born to working-class parents,' he says. 'I was able to graduate into the professional classes. You can lose a bit of touch with your roots. You're so busy just doing your job, your family, so until you come face to face with these very real problems it doesn't affect you, you've got other things to worry about.'

Gordon was more closely involved because costs were vital now in whatever the Building Committee considered. 'We were controlled by the amount of money they had to spend,' Kevin says; and by the time within which decisions were needed. Bill Halsall prepared the working drawings, Gordon Tait the Bill of Quantities. As they went along they got the Building Committee to make the decisions they needed. In the early days the design committees had had some delegated power; Steve Cossack says, 'There was a tacit agreement that, yeh, you've put the graft into it: unless there's anything really controversial, we'll endorse it.' This tacit agreement continued now. So Kevin, Billy Floyd, Philip, Peter and Irene – the hard-core of the building committee – made a number of detailed decisions about the building. Bricks, mortar, tiles, types of windows and doors were selected; samples would go back to the management committee and circulate among the members.

The principle of uniformity, of everyone having the same, persisted. Kevin: 'We stumbled across the idea of having different coloured bricks for different courts. That was going to be it. We said, Hm. We went away and thought about it. No, it's got to be one. Uniform is the answer.' Uniformity would avoid arguments. And, as Kevin says, 'We didn't know about maintenance allowances then. All we wanted to do was, do it in the most uniform fashion so we had the least maintenance.'

The committee also began considering the form of contract they might use with a builder. They looked at ways of cutting the costs if the tenders from contractors came in above the 'yardstick' that had been set up for the scheme.

Philip Roberts was someone who'd been persuaded on to the management committee over the last six months, and had been to a number of building committee meetings. Sammy's son and Arthur's brother, Philip, knew something from them about the way the committees worked. But 'I was getting lost,' he says. 'The nucleus, now they knew what was going on 'cause they'd been on from start to finish. Things were going on, they understood. I asked, and they explained it to me. But they were telling me in five minutes what they'd learned over years. So when something new came up I leapt at it.'

'Something new' was the landscaping committee. The long-standing members of the management committee were still deeply involved in the other business of the co-op; but by the spring of 1980 it was becoming urgent to put together some landscaping ideas, and to start trying to get hold of money to pay for it. Philip recalls: 'I volunteered to go on the committee and a few others – Danny Ford, Sandra Meadows, Ann Byrne, John Grant, Irene Moore. We didn't know nothing about landscaping but we knew bits about gardening. We got talking to the management committee, we got dealing with a landscaping firm, COMTECHSA.'

The Housing Corporation and the Department of the Environment had refused to pay for the services of a landscape architect. So, on Martine's advice, the co-op went to COMTECHSA: a newly formed organization, controlled by the groups it was to provide landscaping and architectural services to. Mike Padmore of COMTECHSA began to come to meetings. He said they'd waive their fees if the co-op couldn't get money together for that. He began to teach the landscaping committee what he knew; they began to organize trips out – very much as the design committees had begun.

Nobody seems to have suggested that BDG might pass on some of their fees in order to employ a landscape architect. Instead, the awkward arrangement with COMTECHSA immediately led to difficulties. After one meeting, Bill Halsall wrote grumpily to the co-op:

> When [COMTECHSA's] involvement was mooted, it was made clear to all parties that they would have to operate as consultants to BDG. From recent discussions with them, there is some suggestion that they want separate design control of some or part of the landscape works. This suggestion is completely unacceptable to BDG...

Billy Floyd and the committee supported Bill Halsall; liaison arrangements were worked out.

Underpinning the design and costing work done by the architect and quantity surveyor, was the detailed administration of the co-op's scheme. Joe Corbett serviced the co-op's committees, dealt with the waiting list, allocations and newsletters; CDS still did the dealings with outside bodies. The main CDS worker with the Weller Streets by now was Martine Gouilleux; Catherine Meredith very rarely came to meetings; Paul Lusk was called in as and when needed. Martine suggested in April that the co-op might like to consider reviewing the development agreement with CDS. The committee, though, was worried that their grant aid for Joe Corbett might not continue: under the new Conservative government, the Housing Corporation's support for co-operatives was under review. So they agreed, the minutes record, 'that the existing Management Agreement should stand. It was also agreed that both parties should agree to proceed with a gradual transfer of administrative responsibility onto the Co-op.'

When Billy Floyd wrote to the Minister of Housing a fortnight later to emphasize the need for grant aid for a worker, he avowed:

> The intention of the Co-operative is that we should eventually become a completely autonomous organization, responsible for

running our own affairs...With the services of a grant-aided worker, we can work towards our goal of establishing a self-sufficient community that will not suffer from vandalism, etc., thereby relieving a burden from the shoulders of the local authority, and the State.

The commitment to CDS was, though, more of a commitment to Martine and Paul Lusk than a commitment to the organization. The distinction between the individuals and the organization that had been there from the beginning still held. And the co-op's involvement in the organization's internal politics was renewed.

The immediate cause of this was Paul in CDS leaking to the co-op that Stephen Rice, the co-op's representative on the CDS management committee, was on the JCC, CDS's management –union negotiating body. That didn't please the union-minded men on the committee. Philip Hughes had joined the co-op with Stephen, but by now had become his arch-critic, seeing Stephen as too closely allied with the 'professionals'. As Philip recalls: 'He had got himself elected on to the JCC. He was on that and we didn't know about it. We found out there was all sorts of arguments about grades and pay. We said, "You keep right out of that shit." He said, "The point is, I'm on it to give the trade union point of view." We said, "It's up to them people to represent themselves." We had more to concern ourselves with than internal struggles within CDS.' Eventually Stephen was removed as the co-op's representative on the CDS management committee.

There was also a confused debate in CDS around this time about their service to co-ops. One prong of this was a proposal for CDS to seek 'charitable status' so that its tenants wouldn't have the 'right to buy' under the new Tory legislation, and so that the organization would have certain tax advantages. The Weller Streets saw the potential threat in this to them: the co-op development arm of CDS's work might have to be hived off to another organization, or dropped altogether. Peter Tyrrell went to an 'open day' on the subject: 'The day that done me was a day in the YMCA. We spent all morning, they had about ten things on the agenda: and all they agreed to was a fucking feasibility study. At one time they were talking about pulling out of co-op development altogether. I said they should change their fucking name: Co-operative Development Services!'

Here a more personal element enters the debate. For it wasn't CDS's 'official' view that charitable status would rule out work with co-ops: it was Martine's personal opinion of the implications. Martine, formerly a close personal friend of Catherine Meredith, was feeling increasingly opposed to what CDS was doing. What began as an argument about Martine getting more staff ended up as an attempt to orchestrate a vote of no confidence in Catherine Meredith at the CDS management committee: an attempt which failed. The Weller Streets waded in in support of Martine: just as they had done before, with Rory Heap and the Toxteth Community Council, with Paul and Martine in CDS in 1978, with Bill Halsall over the design in 1979: they supported the individual they knew to be their 'friend' against the organization.

But predominantly, in the spring and summer of 1980, the co-op had, in Philip's phrase, 'more to concern ourselves with than internal struggles within CDS'. As Joe Corbett puts it: 'The pressure on the co-op for action became much more intense after February 1980, what Billy calls the Burning the Boats meeting.' And in fact much of this pressure was *within* the co-op: from the general members on the committee, to produce what they'd promised.

The general membership wasn't privy to much of the debate about 'professionals', or detailed design. They were presented with the results of the debate: the committee worried a lot about whether the presentation had gone over well. 'I just kept going to meetings,' says Rozzie Lybert. 'I used to come home from the meetings saying, "I'm not going again, I'm bored to tears." Then next month I'd go.'

The fund-raising committee kept up the momentum of functions: every other week the women'd organize a coffee afternoon, or a cheese and wine, or a social. They tried out some more outrageous ideas, as Lily Faulkner remembers: 'Kate, she wanted them sponsoring. They went on a pub crawl Sunday morning: on their knees. They started at Wilkie's: Kate, and Irene Stead, she had those cricket pads on her knees, and Steve Cossack – you know how big he is. But somebody said they shouldn't do it, 'cause we're not a charity.'

The functions helped to involve a wide spectrum of the membership. And the committee worked at putting information across at general meetings, while the allocations of individual houses and flats continued. They got the local primary school involved in making a model of the scheme. Lily Faulkner remembers: 'In the end all the children made all the houses and flats as they were having them, they made them the exact replica of what we were going to. And that's when you knew that that was it, when you picked your number.'

In Lily's view, 'that was it' when you knew where you were going to live, and saw what it'd be like on the model. But the committee knew that wasn't quite it. The co-op didn't yet have a builder. Bill and Gordon drew up a list of seven building contractors: the co-op approved them. In April tenders were invited: the formal approval to do the work Bill and Gordon had in fact spent the last five months doing, at risk, came through on the same day.

'Four weeks later,' as Gordon describes it, 'the tenders were returned, on 20 May. An evening meeting was held, attended by the co-op members, representatives of CDS – Paul Lusk and Martine – Dave Wilkinson and Bill Halsall, and Jack Houghton [Gordon's boss] and myself. Amidst very tense expectations the sealed envelopes were brought out and opened. Five of the tenders received were within the yardstick cost.' Paul Lusk video'd the ceremony for posterity. People were exultant. The fifth-lowest price was just over the cost yardstick in fact, at £1,291,716 – the figures were so huge they were hard to take in – but there were four contractors within the yardstick. Billy Floyd remembers an unexpected contribution to the celebrations: 'Jack Houghton had this fucking great briefcase with him. We all thought it was full of papers and all that. And he opened it up, and there was this bottle of whisky and all these glasses.'

When people recall this period, their memories make it seem to have lasted for months and months; in fact the tenders were considered over a period of a few weeks. The tension and expectation were immense. And within a week the two lowest-priced contractors had dropped out, both claiming they had made large arithmetical errors. A general meeting was imminent. The committee's confidence sagged: they decided to put a brave face on it, as the minutes of the general meeting record:

> The lowest tender had been that of Unit Construction, but after careful thought, it had been decided not to offer them the contract – the Committee had heard that Unit were planning to lay off staff and transfer resources to Scotland – it turned out that Crudens were keen to take on the contract and had tendered a figure of £1,202,169, over £48,000 within the yardstick.

This was 'putting on a front to our own people' with a vengeance: untruths which would have been unacceptable from 'professionals', but which the committee needed to bolster people's confidence – including their own.

Gordon Tait was calm and methodical: the co-op applied for approval to sign a contract with Crudens. At a general meeting in the middle of June Joe Corbett reported confidently on progress with Crudens, in amongst discussion of landscaping proposals and a first debate about what to call the courtyards in the scheme. A week after that, Joe recalls, it all went wrong: 'The crunch one was Crudens in Warrington. Everything was ready, we were simply waiting to meet them to sign the contract. What we got was a phone call to CDS. They announced they didn't want to take the matter any further. We were in the Toxteth pub. Martine and Bill came in looking like messengers of doom.'

They were messengers of doom. Nobody could fathom it. It seemed as if contractors were taking fright at the whole idea of a co-operative. Philip Hughes – known as an inexhaustible joker, as well as the 'pedant' – tried to be jovial, but everybody was plunged in gloom. Bill Halsall was as depressed as the committee: 'All the people involved divided into believers and people who were sitting on the fence. It came to a head when the tenders were coming back and the first on the list were dropping out. That was the blackest hour for me. Before that, there'd always been professional answers. There was always a way of getting round the problem. When it got to that stage there was nothing I knew that could be done about it. It was out of the bureaucratic system and into the market place. It really sunk in then that you either carried on believing in it or you gave up. It got past the level of doing a job. It got to the level of a crusade.'

Suddenly it looked like a crusade that was going to fail. 'Bill's bottle had gone,' as Billy Floyd puts it. And Billy had always relied on Bill to pull a professional answer out of the hat. If he couldn't see a way out of the problem, who could? 'It was gone,' Peter Tyrrell felt. 'The baby was dying, the baby was nearly fucking dead. I felt really pissed off. I don't think the nucleus – me, Kevin, Billy, Phil – we were still determined somebody was going to fucking build it.'

But who? Gordon Tait had approached the fourth-lowest contractor. They'd said they were no longer interested in doing the job. Maybe belief and determination, that had carried them this far, weren't going to be enough. Kitty remembers the atmosphere of the committee: 'That's the time when Billy said, "I've got a ticket for Siberia." We said, "You'd better get nine." I thought, "That's it, no one's going to build the houses." We'd convinced everybody, we'd even told them we had the builders. It was frightening. What were we going to do? Everyone was equally down. I remember talking to Thelma next day and she'd said Billy had come home from the meeting crying, saying, "What are we going to tell the people?"'

The committee decided their promises had gone so far that they couldn't tell the general membership what was happening. 'We couldn't tell members anything,' Joe Corbett says. 'People'd stop you in the street and say they'd heard it was going to be Crudens and you'd say, Mm, yes.' Kitty recalls: 'We were frightened of any of our members stopping us in the street. I remember Mrs Lybert, I said to her, "Yeh, the builders have dropped out but we've got a better one and they're cheaper." She's my auntie, you see, and somehow the word had got out. You'd be trying to keep your tongue between your teeth.'

Gordon Tait approached the fifth-lowest contractor, Tomkinson's, to see if they'd be prepared to do the job. A committee delegation went straight from going to Crudens office to tell them what they thought of them, to meet in Gordon's office to try and find savings that would bring Tomkinson's tender within yardstick.

And in the midst of all this, the first international visitors came to visit the co-op: a delegation of housing people from Third World countries. Arthur Roberts recalls: 'We had a party from all the countries, Indians, Asians, Chinese. I don't think they realized what sort of house we lived in: the toilet at the back and the little stairs.' Vera Large comments: 'One feller said, in some parts of his country what we were living in was palaces compared to what they had.'

Teresa, the landlady at Wilkie's, put on a spread. To committee members entertaining the visitors was both light relief and nightmare. They had to keep up the front that all was well with the co-op. But they also had the opportunity to let their hair down a bit. Ivy Stead recalls: 'They put a meal on at the Crown. They didn't want to go on the coach when it came, they were all rotten [drunk]. The next lot, we gave them a pan of scouse*.' (Ivy's referring to some later visitors. Knowing there were Muslims in the party, the co-op had asked the chef at the Holiday Inn for advice, and had been told that tripe in lettuce leaves would be in order. But when they all came to eat, the visitors demolished the pan of scouse meant for the members, who had to settle for the tripe in lettuce leaves.)

The visit was filmed by Granada Television. Still unsure of whether the co-op would get a building contractor, Billy Floyd was interviewed and put a brave face on it: 'I think the message here,' he said to the cameras, 'is that you can do it if you're determined, and you believe, and you're prepared to go through an education programme which we had to do. We had to go and learn how to do this. But you can, you can beat the system if you really want to.' But could they?

Some of the other professionals tried to keep up morale among the committee members. Paul Lusk says, 'I remember afterwards Billy saying, I'd been the trainer who'd come on with the towel when the boxer was down. I was furious.' Peter Tyrrell particularly remembers the contributions of Martine and Gordon. 'Martine pulled together then; she was a great pillar of strength around that time. She felt the pain as much as us. And she was getting paid for it. She definitely done beyond the call of duty. She was a big coaxer and great believer in your ability: at the time she was of fucking great assistance to us. Every other [professional] was prepared to bury their hands – except Gordon was a cracker. He went away and rewrote the Bills in a day and a half. It changed them, you see. They'd never worked at the same client level before. They'd seen the work that had been put in and they thought, "This'll be fucking tragic if this goes down here."'

*Scouse is the Liverpool stew which gave its name to local people, Scousers, and the local dialect, Scouse.

Gordon kept his head throughout. 'The quantity surveyors were confident,' according to Paul Lusk. In fact, such a wholesale withdrawal of tenders was, Gordon says, 'something unique in my experience of nearly thirty years in the quantity surveying profession'. But he kept up an air of calm. At a general meeting at the end of June not a word was breathed of the problems with the contractors. Instead, 'Bill Halsall of BDG, and Gordon Tait of Houghton & Stackpoole, the Quantity Surveyors, gave an explanatory talk about what would happen when building work began.'

But would it ever begin? There were rumours that the Housing Corporation might be a victim of government spending cuts later in the year; if the co-op had to go out to tender again the scheme might go under. And Tomkinson's, the fifth-lowest contractor, wanted assurances about where the co-op was getting its money from; and a contract period of two years instead of one and a half.

The strain on committee members and those closely involved with them was beginning to tell. Joe Corbett says, 'For a number of weeks it was a very trying time for everybody. I think Philip calls it the dark days of 1980. We all started to hit the bottle quite outrageously. For about a month I hardly ate anything. About all I could manage was a cucumber salad. I just drank. At the end of the month I'd lost a stone in weight and had a bank overdraft.'

Billy Floyd led a deputation of half a dozen, along with Bill, Gordon and Paul, to go and see Tomkinson's. At first they were treated with suspicion: the old problem of convincing people that a load of scallies knew a legitimate way of laying their hands on a million quid. Peter Tyrrell says of Billy and Kevin: 'I thought it was great. They were down to the fucking bones – on their arse. But they never went cap in hand to Tomkie's. Whatever had gone on with anybody else didn't affect them.' It affected them, but didn't dampen the anger they'd kept with them from the beginning, the 'fight'. And in the pub the 'dream' they'd all tried to carry on believing in turned to fantasy. If this builder didn't come through what would they do? One was for burning down the old Weller Streets; another [a professional] for burning down the Builders' Federation: fantasies like that one in the design period of a wall topped with barbed wire and gun turrets round their scheme. But that fantasy had expressed some kind of hope; these, despair.

A group of committee members went to see Max Steinberg at the Housing Corporation to get a letter affirming the co-op were a *bona fide*, government-aided group. The letter came through. A lucky break: the yardstick had increased for inflation during the tender period, so no savings needed to be made. Peter Tyrrell says, 'All Tomkie's were interested in was the fucking money. Once they found the money we could have been Commoes or Greenheads for all they cared.'

But, with the co-op over a barrel, Tomkinson's held out for a two-year contract period. Billy Floyd's affection for Charlie Barnes of the Department of the Environment in Manchester – their mutual affection – bore fruit now. Billy recalls: 'Charlie Barnes in the DoE, he was swinging things for more money and an extension to the contract period and everything. In those days I was needing somebody to bounce off. I used Charlie as a confessor at the time. He was a patient guy. At the time Halsall was gone, he was carried away. I phoned him, I said, "Charlie, I'm at my wits' end, they want a fucking extension of six months to the contract, what am I going to do?" Charlie said, "Well, what are you going to do?" I said, "Well, I suppose I'm going to have to ask Max Steinberg for another six months – I'm doing my best." Charlie said, "If you're doing your best, lad, then that's good enough for me."'

Max Steinberg agreed to the six months extra. He and Charlie Barnes hurried through their approvals. At last, after all the heartache, the building contract could be entered into. Joe Corbett: 'The contract was signed on 5 August. The start on site date in the programme was projected for 4 August. So they weren't far out despite all the uncertainties and delays.' The committee went up to BDG's offices to sign up, armed with litre bottles and an ice bucket. Then everyone adjourned at 4.30 in the afternoon to Wilkie's, where the landlady Teresa had laid on a buffet. Philip went behind the bar: drinks were on the house; the people from Tomkinson's were amazed. And then, as Joe Corbett recalls, 'I remember the next day photocopying the contract and going round with Billy giving it to people, saying, "The worrying's over, folks."'

Why had so many contractors dropped out? 'One can only speculate,' is Gordon Tait's view. 'It may well be that the two lowest did find arithmetical errors in their tenders, it would be a coincidence but it's possible. And the unusual or pioneering nature of this...co-operative: that the nature of the co-op was not fully understood by the contractors: so perhaps there was apprehension, perhaps they thought, "Let someone else do the work." But that's pure speculation.' As Peter Tyrrell puts it: 'We'll never know the truth of what went on there now. You hear things but they've got to stay in your head.'

The committee was drained. Nothing was going to stop the dream now. But business went on. The week after, a general meeting saw a video show of the contract signing done by Paul Lusk, but also decided on a set of draft management proposals for how the estate would be run when it was completed, and expelled another member who'd failed to fulfil the attendance rules. There was hardly time to breathe, to savour the triumph; they had to plunge on into another unknown experience without pause for reflection.

8

A Lot of Little Churches:
Changing Relationships on Site

'It became more interesting', says Rozzie Lybert, 'once the fencing went up. You could actually see it. Before, it was all on paper: a fantasy.' A lot of people felt that: that the co-op only became real once the building started.

But the start on site was an anti-climax. It seemed to take ages for the building to get going. Tom Phillips, the co-op's clerk of works, remembers: 'It was supposed to start the beginning of August. It didn't start till about the October; then when it did start it was dead slow. And the reason, Tomkinson's had a site agent, he was just finishing a job. But he didn't finish his [other] job till the following year.' Tom ended up lending a hand, with the sub-contractor doing the setting out, so that the drains and foundation work could get moving. But at last progress was being made, the works had begun.

Although the co-op had gone through the formalities of interviewing, Tom Phillips was the person Bill Halsall had had in mind for clerk of works from the first. Tom had already worked for BDG for two and a half years. He was in his mid-sixties, with a lifetime's experience in the building trade, as joiner, site agent and unsuccessful contractor.

'One of the agreements,' Tom says, 'was I would attend their meetings if they needed me.' The first committee meeting he went to was in August 1980. 'They'd start a meeting. Everything'd be serious, you know. Then somebody'd come out with some crack or other and everybody'd be laughing. Then they'd be serious again.' At the end of Tom's first meeting there was a bit of horse-play afterwards between two committee members. 'I thought, "Ooh, what have I joined here?" We went for a drink. They said, "You must think we're bloody mad. Well, if we didn't do that sort of thing we would have gone mad. It was only through this sort of thing that we've kept going."'

Tom had recently lost his wife after forty years of marriage. He found it hard to get involved. 'I'd come home here to nothing. One day I said to myself, "I've got to get out of this depression." I thought, the only way to do it is to join these comedians. That's what I did. I joined them in everything they were doing. Everything changed from then.' Tom became another paid worker who got personally involved with the co-op.

While most of the fighting was over once the contractor was on site, the Building Committee still had a lot of details to sort out, about fitments and finishes. The committee – Kevin, Billy, Irene, Peter and Philip – went through some of the familiar arguments about choice against uniformity. Kevin says, 'Bill Halsall – he wanted to have different [coloured] doors. We said, "One colour, that's it." It was important to us, that everyone had the same. I put it down to basic human jealousies, 'cause if I had a red door and somebody else had a green door and theirs looked a little bit better...' Kevin doesn't remember any of the older people talking about the old days before the war, when the houses were all painted the same and people helped each other out, but some of the idea must have sprung from that, as well as some of the popular support from general members not closely involved in the design process.

Kevin was full of ideas over the details. He managed to convince Bill Halsall and then the others that doors and woodwork should be left with a natural wood look. It was agreed there could be a limited choice of stains. Peter Tyrrell recalls: 'The funniest meetings were over the stains. People wanted all sorts of different ones. Me Kevin and Philip kept saying we were having 08, 09, 10. Other people were putting forward other things. We convinced them in the end.'

Some of the old conflict about who this 'we' was that convinced 'them' came back to the surface in these design debates. Philip Hughes recalls: 'We had a certain meeting and Irene wouldn't talk to us one night 'cause she thought it'd all been sorted out in the pub. As it happens I hadn't had a drink that night.' But in general the point was true: 'a lot of the thinking', in Philip's phrase, was still done in Wilkie's. Kitty and Irene in particular felt excluded by the men because of this: 'We used to think the men were making little of us,' Kitty says, and while she accepts that 'you couldn't just switch it off when you went to the pub', still it meant that some committee members knew more of what was going on than others.

Yet Kitty and Irene were still heavily responsible for liaising between the committee and the general membership on design. Bill Halsall, for instance, recalls: 'There was an amazing degree of unanimity on a lot of things to do with the detail. We had a big argument at one stage about kitchen units. Kevin wanted everybody to have the same colour kitchen units. I was saying it wouldn't cost any more, it wouldn't cause any delay to have a choice. The committee decided on two choices of door colour, two choices of worktop colour. A questionnaire was done. Almost everybody chose the same thing.' Within this process Irene was supporting Bill in pressing for choice; she and Kitty were doing the questionnaires; and the 'amazing degree of unanimity' was connected with the women's network on the streets, fed with information by Kitty and Irene.

There were also general meetings where the progress of the detailed design was explained. Billy Lybert: 'We chose the colour of the units, and the doors. Of course, we couldn't have gold bars on the windows, like – but whatever anybody asked for was noted. It all got noted down. He'd tell you what was available. Y'see, I've got skirting boards and surrounds in white; some have got stains. Them meetings went very well.'

Or Lily Faulkner recalls: 'They used to put it on the screen. Bill gave us a lecture one night. He showed us all the locks – these windows. Then he brought the windows down to show us.' This was how the general members saw the design: progress being reported to them periodically, with some degree of choice over details.

So committee members were still busy, but, with the contract signed, were at last able to relax a little for the first time for three years. 'Once the security fencing went up and the contractors' compound had been erected,' Gordon Tait says, 'everybody breathed a sigh of relief.' The fighting for land, money and recognition was over; the time for spadework, in all senses, had come. The strain on committee members had been enormous, and had touched their private lives. As far back as 1978 Rory Heap remembers it being discussed: 'How do we involve our families in what we're doing? Or do we stay in the co-op and get divorced? With five meetings a week?' Committee members often spent more time at meetings, or in pubs discussing the meetings, than they did at home. Kitty remembers: 'Me and my husband'd have row after row. He was fed up of me not being in. I think everyone on the committee went through that. But we were determined that the people who were in at the beginning were the people who were going to make it succeed.' The intensity of this had helped to cause some, like Harry Dono and Billy Odger, to leave altogether; some to have periods of not being so closely involved; some to stick with it and have the rows. Inevitably friendship and affection developed among the inner group of committee members and professionals, and that too rebounded back on people's home lives.

Different couples approached the problem in different ways. Some spouses were involved themselves in one committee or another: Ann Byrne on the management committee at first, later on fund-raising and landscaping; Margaret Hughes on the Inside committee; Thelma Floyd on fund-raising. Others preferred to stay in the background. But whether spouses were deeply involved in the co-op or not, they certainly made a major contribution in their patience and their child- and home-minding.

Of all the personal pressure that had fallen on committee members, perhaps the greatest had fallen on Billy Floyd as chairman. Everyone in or involved with the co-op agrees that, while the co-op depended on a substantial group of people to make it work, it was Billy who led and guided them to the goal of getting houses on site. He chaired meetings; led deputations here, there and everywhere; was widely regarded among the co-op membership as the one to go to if you had a problem; had cajoled, connived and pushed behind the scenes. As Stephen Rice puts it: 'I've seen a lot of managers. I rate him as the best I've ever seen. I honestly believe he could go and manage a football team and make them better. He can motivate people. Like Churchill he was a warmonger; he was all right while the battle was going on; in peacetime maybe somebody else should lead.'

Billy himself came to the conclusion that it was time for a change. In October, when the building was getting going on site, he approached Peter Tyrrell. As Peter recounts: 'I never envisaged anyone except Billy being chairman. When you come to the reasons why it changed, it was another fucking good move on Billy's part. Billy was a great motivator. He'd seen that part was over now. It needed something a bit subtler, a bit more gentle persuasion now – going through the procedures. It was a Sunday night. He come round to our house with Joe. "I've decided you're going to be the fucking chairman," he said. The man was drained with the amount of effort he'd put into it. It was a miracle he was fucking standing.'

Peter Tyrrell had, like Billy, tended from early on to go to as many meetings of the co-op as he could, just to see and contribute to what was going on. He'd been a union shop steward in Lairds at one time and again, more recently, as a schools caretaker. He was cagier, less of an extrovert than Billy. And his work, split into different shifts during the day, meant he could be available at various times. He realized that would help the chairman's job now: 'It needed somebody who could be on site a lot. I could be down here twice or three times a day. He had the foresight to see that, Billy. I think I had the same hardline attitude as him, you know, they've got to fucking do it.' But as Joe Corbett recalls Billy's resignation, 'The committee wouldn't accept it at first: some people understood him to be resigning from the co-op.' In the end, when they realized that wasn't so, and that he'd be prepared to stay on the committee itself, they reluctantly accepted his decision.

The committee itself had undergone a number of changes now. In the summer of 1980 Eifion Wynn-Jones had been expelled. He accepted it philosophically; he'd left temporarily to go down south: 'I was one of those who made the rule that if anybody left the co-op they'd have to hand in their share.'

Stephen Rice's attendance at committee meetings had begun to dwindle during 1980. 'I think what put the top hat on him,' says Kitty, 'was that he was too close with CDS.' After the row over what he was doing on CDS's management committee as Weller Streets rep, CDS kept him on their committee as an 'individual member'. He became more closely involved with the 'professionals' than with the co-op. He'd always been, as Sue Jackson puts it, 'quite different from the Weller Streets people'. Or, in Arthur Roberts' view: 'He did a lot of good things but he got up a few people's noses. He always wanted to buy his own house but he wanted to help set this whole thing up.'

A lot of people found that hard to understand. Peter Tyrrell says: 'He'd already intimated...I'm doing all this for you and I'm not going to live down there. I could never understand, if he wasn't going to live down there, why he didn't just resign his share and do whatever he was going to do.'

A number of the men had been in it more for the fight, for the idea, than for the prospect of a house at the end of it. But Stephen Rice was the only one who said, 'I'm not coming with you.' In the autumn of 1980 he stopped coming to committee meetings at all. 'They had a rule,' Kitty recalls, 'if committee members didn't come to four meetings they had a letter saying they were off the committee.' In January 1981 Stephen got his letter. 'It went to two months before he even got that letter. They give him leeway. If I leave the committee I'll send in a letter saying I'm resigning. If I got a letter, I wouldn't get a cob on, 'cause I'd know they'd be right.'

That's Kitty's view. It caused a row between Kitty and Ann Caddis, Stephen's sister, a few weeks later, even though Kitty admired him for sticking with the co-op when he wasn't going to move in. But by then Stephen with his wife had already moved to a house of their own in Dovecot, hurt by his dismissal after all the work he'd put in.

At the same time as these departures, other people were joining the committee. One was Keith Lewis, who'd only recently moved into the area. 'We moved in to my ex-wife's grandmother's house, knowing we'd get something.' Keith had originally assumed the 'something' would be Corpie rehousing. Then he'd heard about the co-op. 'I just went along to show my face really, to get something out of it. Then I did actually get interested in it.'

New members of the committee faced again some of the problems committee members not in the 'inner group' had faced before. As Keith describes it: 'Quite rightly the people who started it off was a bit of a clique. They were coming to the committee saying "We decided . . ." 'cause they'd talked about it in the pub.' For, besides the new faces like Keith Lewis and Billy Lybert, and the return of familiar ones – Steve Cossack, Pat Russell – the old hard-core of the committee was still there.

And there was Dickie Sharp. 'A stalwart and a gentleman to boot: my staunchest ally,' says Stephen Rice of him. Dickie was a quiet, modest man, capable of getting on with opposing factions even when they were falling out with each other. Nominally he was the treasurer; in practice he was Lord High Everything Else for the co-op, keeping up with the subs, helping out with people's problems, running around, and always at the meetings. 'To the old,' Peter Tyrrell says, 'he was looked upon as the fucking boss of the co-op. He was so good at dealing with people.'

Dickie was one of those who was increasingly concerned, over the winter of 1980/1, at the conditions in the Weller Streets. By February 1981 it was twelve months since the Corporation had been round to talk to people about rehousing. It seemed as if the Corporation was rehousing non-co-op-members unusually quickly. More and more houses were getting boarded up. Vandalism and break-ins were on the increase. Edie McLennan recalls: 'We'd get knocks on our door. If it was one of our neighbours they'd lift the letter box and say, "It's only Ann."' Her husband Joe: 'We got that way we wouldn't get out.' The older people in the community were frightened and nervous. 'Where we were,' Lily Durrant says, 'the houses were gradually getting ruined at the back of us, the roofs were off.' Her sister Ada Hewitt says: 'It's a time we never thought we'd live through. They had me on the TV. My nephews had made iron bars on the windows.'

So in February the committee approached CDS and two other housing associations to see if they could offer temporary rehousing: for the builders would be finishing the houses in 'phases', and some wouldn't be ready for another eighteen months. Only CDS said they were able, in principle, to help, provided people were 'in need', and that houses would be licensed rather than rented to co-op members, so CDS could be sure they'd leave when their co-op house was ready.

While matters like this meant that the committee was still

busy, in general the greater breathing space they had, once the houses were on site, gave them room to look outw rds a bit more. In the autumn of 1980 they began to have close dealings with the other co-ops that had begun to develop in Liverpool.

The Weller Streets had already had some dealings with other co-ops before then. From 1979, Paul Lusk had begun to use them to talk to other groups that approached CDS. He accepts: 'Once they got big they were used...I was very keen we should use the Weller as a demonstration project, the model, the teachers for others. That meant pestering the Weller to do a lot of things they didn't really want to do. It was something that has to be laid at my door, that Weller should become this kind of lighthouse.' The other co-ops they met seemed quite a lot different from the Weller Streets. Peter Tyrrell says his impression was that 'That same keenness wasn't there, for us, that we seemed to have. They seemed to want just a house really. They'd get a bit of land then let somebody else run it for ever. We'd seen this could be a fucking dinosaur.' The 'dinosaur' intended to become self-managing; other co-ops seemed to expect to depend on professional support for ever. And the pressure to give pep talks to such groups came when there was a lot of pressure within the co-op too. Paul Lusk says, 'I nagged them, personally or through Martine. It's like having a gifted child you flog to death.'

When the 'gifted child' took stock, in the autumn of 1980, it didn't like what the parent was doing. The new wave of co-ops got their money from the Liberal–Tory ruling alliance on the Council, not from the Housing Corporation. Most of them were Corporation tenants trying to get into new houses: their 'housing need' was less urgent than the need of the Weller Streets members living in clearance. Indeed, when the Weller Streets got involved with the new Liverpool Federation of Housing Co-ops in late 1980, they felt most fellow feeling with other co-ops from clearance areas. 'We did meet some good ones,' Peter Tyrrell says, 'Thirlmere and Leta/Claudia –

especially Thirlmere: Cummings [their chairman], his attitude was fucking right: Let's go to the people who've done it. Any crap he got off anybody, he used to come and see me or Billy. Then he'd go back, and they'd done it the way we done it.'

The Weller Streets' idea of how co-ops together should engage in political lobbying was aggressive and uncompromising. In November 1980 they invaded a private dinner party hosted by Hugh Cubitt, then Chairman of the Housing Corporation, at the Atlantic Tower Hotel, to protest at possible cuts to housing co-operative schemes. Sammy Roberts recalls, 'Eight of us went in, we had to force our way in. He was just getting the soup. One of our members put his finger in it. He said, "You won't eat that, will you? It's contaminated. That's what our places are: contaminated."'

In contrast, the Weller Streets felt that the professionals were prepared to make quiet deals behind closed doors. CDS's view of politics seemed to be 'to play along with the Liberals'; theirs to take on, and seek support from, all comers.

This clash of style with CDS showed up, too, in the way the co-op's administration had progressed. Peter Tyrrell says, 'They were supposed to advise us how to handle the bureaucratic minefield but they became bureaucrats themselves. They couldn't handle us saying, this is how we want to do it . . . I think in the end CDS were prepared to let it grind its way through the fucking machinery. We had to kick it up the arse and do it ourselves.' Kitty feels, 'They were supposed to do things themselves and never did it. Billy Floyd and a couple of others ended up doing the dirty work they should have been doing.'

Everyone recalls Catherine Meredith's undertaking to come to committee meetings every fortnight, which lapsed in 1979. Martine had become the only regular attender of co-op meetings by the time of the building contract. Like Sue Jackson four years before, people saw her less and less as somebody from CDS, more and more as an individual working with the co-op. So CDS weren't coming to meetings, but Martine was. And maybe people in the co-op had forgotten that they'd told CDS not to go to certain meetings, and blamed CDS for things that the co-op had actually taken out of CDS's hands.

The 'objective' side of the growing discord between the co-op and CDS is, anyway, fogged by personal issues. Martine had come to feel more and more personally identified with the Weller Streets. She came to share their view that, of the groups CDS worked with, they were the only 'real co-op': just as Paul Lusk had felt in 1978, and had encouraged the Weller Streets to believe. In Philip Hughes' view, 'She got to like drinking with a load of rascals, and moved to the other side.' Finally, in March 1981, she resigned from CDS; Catherine Meredith refused to accept her resignation. She regarded Martine's involvement in the attempted vote of no confidence in her, Martine's increasing disinclination to work with other co-ops, and now her attempts to resign as 'Martine having personal problems that needed helping'.

All these strands – CDS's way of working, the different kind of co-ops they were working with, and the personal issues – came together at the end of March, when Paul Lusk came with another CDS worker to talk to the management committee at their request about a CDS paper on 'local authority co-ops.' These were management co-ops involving Council tenants taking over some of the management of their existing housing. Catherine Meredith says, 'We had written a report for the local authority... because we'd been asked to do so. We were keen to try and spread the message; keen to get a foothold with local authority tenants. All our stuff had provisos about the unions, etc.'

This was politically controversial. The Weller Streets were strongly against the idea. Peter Tyrrell says: 'We wanted no part of that. CDS wanted to help people to get involved in assisting the Corpie to manage their fucking shite. Luskie came up with all sorts of [reasons] for that.' The meeting got personal too. Paul felt the mood was 'vicious, more ugly than before'. The 'atmosphere of menace' that had originally helped to attract him to the co-op now faced him across the table. 'The first surprise', he says, 'was Martine being there, sitting in the corner taking notes, then all these accusations. It was Martine's work I was being criticized for.'

How much Martine contributed to this paper is one of those things obscured by the personal acrimony which followed. Certainly her initials were on the report, together with Paul's and Catherine's; certainly she was now 'on the other side', wanting no part of it. 'That helped to gee up the split,' Peter Tyrrell says. 'How his head stayed on his shoulders that night over that fucking document – We said, let's go boys, let's go now.'

But actually the split was already in hand. Paul Lusk's part in the meeting ended when Billy Floyd held up a note for Chairman Peter Tyrrell – which Paul saw – saying TELL HIM TO FUCK OFF SO WE CAN TALK ABOUT THE NEW SECONDARY. The Weller Streets were planning to set up their own 'secondary co-op' to provide services to other co-ops, in rivalry with CDS.

So Martine insisted she wanted to leave CDS; she did so. She began to work for the Weller Streets for nothing. A few weeks later, at the end of April, CDS got formal notice from the Weller Streets that the co-op wanted to terminate their development agreement. Negotiations began about how much money CDS were owed. According to Peter Tyrrell, 'the split wasn't as amicable as it should have been. That was CDS, they wanted to bleed the baby to death. In the end we sat down and had a meeting and came down to the figure we put forward in the first place.'

In fact the co-op agreed to a little more; and CDS remember the financial details as fairly straightforward. But the mood of the discussions was angry. Keith Lewis recalls: 'One of the fellers there turned round and said to Billy, "Look sonny." And Billy said, "Don't you call me sonny" – I mean, what were they doing? They were sending Martine down and she was on our side in the end, not theirs. They wanted too much credit for what we'd done.'

This was the atmosphere in which they then disputed who had a right to the files in CDS's offices. Catherine Meredith says: 'The battle about the files...was the only one I fought with them on principle. They stormed Bold Street. It was absolutely awful. They phoned up and said they were coming to get their files. They were supposed to have kept their files all along...I don't know why they wanted them...There'd been an exchange of solicitors' letters by this time. It was so easy to set us up being baddies. I said to Kitty who was the only person I felt I could trust, "They're not yours, they're ours. You can have copies of anything you lost." Then it became a prolonged legal battle.' The familiar co-op style, of turning up unannounced, and in aggressive fashion, was turned on their former agents. As Peter Tyrrell sees it: 'They were really keeping hold of our property...We wanted to say, here's the fucking split, give us our records. And we'd have ended up with a relationship with CDS. But what we got in the end was a load of fucking hassle. We ended up hassling in the only way we knew how, and that was going down and demanding them...The whole crux of the matter was, we took Martine away from them. If they'd said that – you could see, it was thinly veiled – we'd have said, fair enough, it's a fucking labour market, let's employ the best there is.'

The split was inevitable at some time or other: the Weller Streets had always intended to be self-managing in the end. Martine's changing 'sides' made the mood of it far sourer than it would have been otherwise. It ended up happening suddenly rather than gradually, and the general membership never therefore understood what went on. 'Any co-op needs someone like that at the beginning,' Kate Kelly concludes philosophically. 'Then you pick their brains and do it yourself.' Other members had only a vague understanding of what was going on. For instance, Ivy Stead, when asked why the co-op split from CDS, said, 'I don't know. They said they were going to break up from CDS and go our own way.' Joe McLennan: 'Instead of letting them do what they wanted to do, CDS wanted to do it themselves...I think CDS wanted to overrule them. I'm only surmising.'

Out of this atmosphere the secondary co-op was born.* The Weller Streets loaned some money to the secondary to get it going. It wasn't universally welcomed by long-standing committee members: Kitty and Philip both voted against setting it up, and Kevin abstained. Enough, though, were enthusiastic: Billy, Peter, Steve Cossack, Keith Lewis.

But within a few months the initiative had petered out. The group's statement of intent set out its stall on being an anti-professional alternative to the likes of CDS, its stated aims (summarized) were:

1. To encourage co-operative housing.
2. To offer mutual support between co-ops and strengthen the movement.

By;

(a) Offering Weller Streets' experience to other co-operatives.
(b) Teaching co-operatives how to become self-sufficient.
(c) Providing an alternative style of education with co-op members teaching one another.

The detailed text of this Statement suggests, however, that the Weller Streets still had something to learn in terms of communication. It's wordy and difficult to follow. For instance, (a) above is explained in detail as follows:

* A 'primary' co-op is one like the Weller Streets, which does work directly for its members. A 'secondary' co-op is made up of a number of 'primaries', for whom it provides services.

Offering other co-operatives the lessons of benefit from Weller Streets Co-operative's experience and success as a working-class group of people in learning from professional experts whilst using the advice and knowledge acquired to produce the co-operative's own independent solutions and to achieve autonomy.

Stephen Rice or Joe Corbett would have done it better: but Stephen had left, and Joe was insecure in his job because the grant aid had been withdrawn. Joe recalls: 'I remember being at a meeting where...they gave me three months' notice. In the next breath Peter asked Martine whether she wanted to work for the Weller Streets and they'd pay her out of management allowances.'

The secondary's efforts at communicating with other co-ops in person didn't go well, either. They had a dry run at a co-ops' fair in Leeds. Peter Tyrrell says, 'We clashed again with professional bodies there. They still had the thing that it couldn't be done without them. We said, "It can be done without you. You're just development agents; we can run it ourselves." They had this attitude they were all Joan of Arcs. They give you the impression they're doing it for fuck-all when they're getting fourteen grand.' But Steve Cossack adds, about that day: 'On reflection we must have come over as a crowd of fascists. We were all drunk.'

The Weller Streets' aggressive style didn't go down well with other co-ops. Only Thirlmere Co-op, also a group of people in a clearance area, showed interest. Paul Lusk says, 'There was this thing about the others not being real co-ops, how we were all in the Liberals' pocket.' This wasn't just the Weller Streets' view; it was broadly the view of socialists and Labour councillors. But the secondary couldn't get going without working with these other co-ops, 'real' or not. As Keith Lewis concludes: 'The idea with the secondary co-op was to be more of a guide – like CDS but better. Again that was just too much work involved. People weren't turning up from other co-ops when we had meetings.' Ironically this was in June/July 1981 when co-ops were snowballing in Liverpool. Paul Lusk says, 'The faster bricks went on the Weller Streets' site, the more people came to us and other people, to say, "How do we do it?" And those people were local people who knew what the Weller Streets had done, who probably had a relative in the Weller Streets.'

The secondary also struggled for support within the Weller Streets' membership. Peter recalls: 'We never got the commitment we thought we would get, mainly from our own. In hindsight it was a bit too soon. At the time I had the impression, let's strike while the iron's hot.' The secondary was finally killed off by a more private scandal. 'Someone was going to fall by the wayside,' says Peter Tyrrell, 'through being together, and all the pressure.' Martine stopped working for the Weller Streets shortly afterwards. Although the Weller Streets had set out their stall on not needing professional support, the secondary proved to be over-dependent on one or two individuals and an unpaid professional who was an administrator rather than a communicator.

The committee's dealings over the secondary were remote from the general membership. They were more concerned with the conditions they were living in, and the conditions they were going to live in once the estate was finished. Despite the row over the development agreement, CDS made fourteen houses available for 'temporary decanting'. The co-op decided that the people whose houses would be finished last would get first choice. Both CDS and the co-op are proud of the correct way they dealt with that. Joe Corbett: 'The co-op played a very straight game on that one.' Catherine Meredith: 'I suppose it was one thing that we stuck with to assure ourselves we weren't being irrational and uncooperative.' So Dickie, Peter and Joe helped people move in in the summer of 1981.

And after the intitial slow progress on site, the building work began to pick up from October/November 1980. The only problem with the site that emerged was what Gordon Tait describes as 'What came to be known as the black hole: a hole filled with black slimy silt, located between two bore holes, which had to be dug out and back-filled with hard-core.'

Tom Phillips settled into his job as clerk of works, and into being, as one member puts it, 'totally infected with the whole idea'. Tom recalls how well he got on with Bill Halsall: 'He's a cracking chap. He's absolutely dead straight which makes a lot of difference in this game...He'll back me up if there's something wrong on the site...and he won't budge, you know.' Bill Halsall had learnt, and grown in confidence, along with the co-op; his relative inexperience didn't show.

Tom settled, too, into a relationship with Tomkinson's site agent, John Bancroft. Tom recalls: 'When we were getting to know each other, he was telling me about his life and I was telling him about mine. He said one of his girls was married and living in Huyton. He said she lives in a lovely house....So he told me the name of the road and I said, "You think they're good houses?" He said, yes, so I said, "I tell you what, John, that's the way I want these houses – 'cause I was the site agent on those houses your daughter lives in."'

Tom popped regularly into people's houses for a chat and a drink; he came to fund-raising dos. The co-op had a party when the first roof went on, and he remembers: 'The men working on the site, they didn't know much about these people. They had a spread on the site: plenty to eat and drink. I think they must have thought, these people are bloody lunatics. We finished all the eats and the ale. Then we went to the pub to finish off. There was one there, she started stripping in the pub. This young bricklayer was trying to take this G-string off with his teeth.'

Tom enjoyed the festive side of the co-op himself; he became known as Kestrel from the lager he drank. But he also became a fierce defender of the standards the co-op had a right to expect. It wasn't easy to keep control of this, with the amount of sub-contracting that Tomkinson's did. Talking to John

Bancroft one day, Tom recalls: 'He said, "What the hell are we building here – a cathedral or something?" And I said, "No, you're building a lot of little churches."'

People used to come down regularly to see how their 'little churches' were getting on. Joe McLennan is one of many: 'We used to come down here many a time, unbeknownst to anybody. I used to say to Edie, it'd be years and years. Then next week there'd be more bricks up. When we come to Leo's [supermarket] we used to come down the back way and have a look.' There were talks from Gordon Tait and Bill Halsall about where things were up to, 'just', says Joe Corbett, 'to reassure people there was light at the end of the tunnel.' Members of the building committee would come and look at progress. Kevin became the co-op's representative at site meetings: he was as obsessed as ever. And there were organized visits for the general membership, as Joe Corbett describes: 'The first conducted site visit was January 1981. It was very important, particularly through that part of the year where the reality of living in the Weller Streets is driven home to you 'cause of the weather, to get them down on site and see what was going on. For most of us it was a learning process again. You see a building topped out and you think, we'll move in next week. It takes almost as long to finish the inside of a building as to put the bricks up.'

Joe himself had moved into the Weller Streets area to live, soon after starting to work for the co-op in 1979. In 1980 he'd applied to go on the waiting list, and had been offered a share later that year. Living in a house Arthur Roberts had lived in, this meant that the co-op would be rehousing from the same house twice: something the Council wouldn't have done if they'd been doing the rehousing.

Although Joe's membership of the co-op, and his living in the area, reinforced his commitment, it also made for difficulties. People saw the hours Dickie Sharp and Peter Tyrrell put in, in their own time, and wondered why they were paying Joe when he was a member too. 'When he produced, it was good work,' says Peter Tyrrell, 'but he was lazy. And we never kicked him up the arse often enough.' This was a rod the committee had made for their own backs. They had a duty to their employee, even if they had subsequently made him a member. It was some of this lack of clarity between 'voluntary' and 'paid' work that helped to lead to Joe getting his notice in mid-1981, when the grant aid ran out. But then when Martine left, he was re-employed, and this time at higher, local authority rates of pay. The awkwardness of his status, though, and the old charges of laziness, dogged his work for the co-op.

Apart from administration Joe put a lot of work, during the contract period, into, as he recalls, 'getting the membership to agree the management policies of the co-op. We had general meetings every fortnight.' This was the eventual follow-up to the rules game: writing up the co-op's tenancy agreement. The rules are simple and straightforward. They're more legalistic than most housing associations' or trendier Councils': concentrating on DOs and DON'Ts rather than on the overall responsibilities of each party. This derives from their origins in the question-and-answer game. The overall philosophy of the co-op is written between the lines, emerging only occasionally in matters like the minor repairs being the responsibility of each household, and that the rules themselves can only be changed by a referendum of the whole membership.

The ideas behind the rules are unusual. As they're expressed in a letter to the Rent Officer* in July 1981:

> Self-management will mostly be organized around the activities of individual courts, with each group of people co-operating amongst themselves. The overseeing and overall control of management and maintenance will remain with our management committee.

---

*The Rent Officer sets 'fair rents' as part of the government grant system.

A representative from each court, a 'court rep', would deal with repair problems; the court reps would change each year so that responsibility would be spread around the co-op and everybody would be involved. This idea was, in a way, built into the design, rather than something which could come out of the later discussion. The courts, 'intimate, private, tucked away' would have to be the focus of the management if everybody was to be involved.

The naming of the courts provoked lively discussion. Edie McLennan recalls: 'Some of them wanted to call them after the Liver docks, some suggested the old neighbourhood streets, someone said flowers. But the trees got it.' One or two of the future residents of 'Palm Court', with memories of Max Jaffa, took a while to get used to the name, but finally accepted it. And the co-op had to find a name for the main access road. It was the City Engineers who'd make recommendations to councillors about whatever name the co-op put forward; people still remembered the meeting over the red and green tarmac. Some years before, Paul Lusk had chalked 'The Weller Way' on a wall, to be photographed for a tape-slide show. That was the name the co-op decided on. The engineers replied:

> However I feel Weller Way would not be appropriate for obvious reasons, and I would therefore suggest Weller Court or Close.
>
> I also consider it unnecessary to name all the courtyards, but simply number the majority of properties off the main access road...

The Weller Streets still had to fight to name their own estate the way they wanted:

> The names were drawn up and agreed by the general members of the co-operative. As the future tenants of the Miles/Byles Street estate, they feel that the court names they have selected

provide the scheme with a distinctive identity...

The Weller Streets got their way in the end.

All this – the naming, the deciding management policies, the site visits – created an atmosphere of high expectation among the membership. But the builders never caught up on their slow start. The first handovers were late. In October 1981, Tom Phillips recounts, 'We started handing the houses over. We had a lot of problems there. Every handover there, they were behind. The first one must have been three or four months behind. And the Weller Streets people, they were living under such terrible conditions that they couldn't get in there quick enough.' Because of the pressure, properties were handed over with snags not dealt with that perhaps should have been mopped up before people moved in.

But handovers fulfilled the dream that people had been watching enacted before their eyes. Billy Lybert: 'We'd all come down on a Sunday. You could see how all the bits you wanted were falling into place.' For the first group of courts there was a celebration at the United Services club, round the corner from the new estate. Lily Faulkner: 'I'll never forget the dance. They called your name out to get the key. And I got halfway across the dance floor and I broke out crying.' Billy Lybert recalls the same occasion: 'I had to go on stage and get our name called out and got the key. That was just the evening. We had to give the keys back, and I didn't want to, like. We all moved in the next day. There were people carrying furniture from halfway down Miles Street.'

A lot of members recall the help Dickie Sharp gave to everyone, especially the pensioners. Ivy Stead: 'Nothing was too much trouble for that man. He came to me the morning I was moving, at seven o'clock. He'd undone the gas cooker, he stayed with me till the van come. He said, "Don't look back" – 'cause you were full up, you know, leaving it all behind. You never heard him say a wrong word about anybody.'

The problems with the building weren't over when people moved in, though. There were snags to be sorted out, and that caused difficulties. Tom Phillips remembers one incident, when the plasterers were called in to deal with some cracks. 'At the time they had no carpet 'cause the people 'd been told [not to]. These plasterers were mixing their plaster on the back, then walking into the house – such a mess – they said, "What difference does it make? They've nothing on the floors. They've not got good furniture. They've got nothing" – That got under my skin. We've all got what we can afford. So we had a right row over that.'

It was to be another twelve months before the last members moved in. Through the whole period of the building contract, the landscaping committee worked on its proposals. In the summer of 1980 the committee had begun learning from Mike Padmore of COMTECHSA the basics of landscaping. As with the design, there were a number of trips out for the whole co-op, to Ness Gardens, Bodnant and other gardens in Merseyside, so people could have a look at plants and trees, and get ideas for their own estate.

Money was a problem from the beginning. Philip Roberts, chairing the committee, says: 'I think it all boiled down to cash.' There was some money allowed by the Housing Corporation within the contract; the co-op managed to get small sums off the Tree Council and the Housing Associations Charitable Trust. But cash was tight. And the co-op got caught in a Catch 22 with the Department of the Environment. On the one hand, while accepting the idea of the design, they wouldn't allow enough through ordinary grant; on the other hand, when the co-op tried to get money through the Urban Programme the DoE said no because 'The project comprises internal landscaping as part of a new housing development...which would largely benefit the occupiers of the housing.'

But there were also problems of communication. Phil says, 'Mike Padmore, he did explain 75 per cent of it; the other 25 per cent was in his head.' The landscaping committee didn't have on it any of the old hands from the design committee. They more readily accepted guidance from Mike Padmore and Bill Halsall, while Bill himself was preoccupied with the building process. 'Them two always used to talk together. So when a meeting came up...there was something about flagstones. They said, "We've already sorted that out." It came to me after, they shouldn't have been doing that. I should have opened my mouth.' And quite apart from the usual problems of jargon, the committee had to grapple with the convention that plants and shrubs are usually referred to by their Latin names. So plans had to be translated for members to understand.

Nevertheless a lot of the co-op's ideas did go into the landscaping. The basic idea was the 'village' feeling; and to break up the uniformity of the courtyards by having different landscaping in each one. They picked trees: mostly medium-sized, flowering cherries and others; and two oaks, for which there's a friendly bet with Bill Halsall as to which'll last longer – the oaks, or the houses.

The committee developed ideas for the planting of the courtyard areas, and brought them to meetings in each court. The time-scale of landscaping was hard to understand. You build a house and it's built; you plant landscaping and it gradually matures over five, ten, fifty years. Phil Roberts says, 'People were seeing – they were expecting instant greenery. They were saying, "You can't have a 25-foot tree in front of your house." I said, "When you get it it'll be about 8 foot and as thick as your finger."'

The committee aimed, in general, for a 'layering' effect, with shrubs and bushes of different heights. Most people wanted a mixture of evergreens and flowers. There would be climbing plants in front of each house, and hanging plants over the walkways between courts on pergolas – wooden battens stretched overhead.

One thing the co-op couldn't afford was low railings around the landscaping in each courtyard. Costs too ruled out the idea of a 3-foot brick wall at the backs of the houses with hedges growing behind. Instead they plumped for 6-foot slatted wooden fencing, so you could see out of the back garden more easily than you could see in.

As each court was completed the landscaping proposals were finalized with the future residents of the court. There were communication problems again. What got planted wasn't what everyone thought they'd agreed to. Phil says: 'When I saw the plans I didn't know the Latin names. So I thought, everything we've agreed to is there. But when they've actually done the planting – he's put a species of nurse plant, one's called buddleia. We never asked for buddleia, but we wanted nurse plants. If he'd have come, like in here [to Phil's house] and explained – but he was always pushed for time.'

Most members, though, were less concerned about the landscaping than with the fact that their houses and flats were being completed. The last ones were handed over in October 1982. Before that, in the summer, Dickie Sharp had fallen ill. Says Peter Tyrrell: 'Dickie was doing everything. He was running the decant rents, manning the office...there was hardly nothing that Dickie wasn't doing...He told me once, he was very pleased, he was amazed, in the times when the young were supposed to be all reckless, that here was a lot of young ones around him who were prepared to get off their arse and do things for the betterment of people.' But Dickie died before his own flat was ready; he never saw his own flat completed, on the estate where he'd helped so many others.

One other of the early committee members didn't get to take up their house: Pat Russell. Peter Tyrrell says of him: 'Pat was a pearler. Pat made a better contribution than some of the people that live down here...Pat done three or four meetings a week, running around in his car to fucking places. He was the unfortunate one, Pat went 'cause of domestic problems.' The way 'domestic problems' become general knowledge is the other side of the coin from the 'neighbourliness' everyone praises. Harry Dono, for instance, quotes an advantage of the estate he's moved to: 'Where I am you don't live in each other's pockets. You did there. You had an argument with your missus, it was in the shop window the next day.'

But for most people, their move into the new homes was a cause for celebration. In October 1982 a carnival was held to celebrate the opening of the last court. The fund-raising committee decided to return to the theme of the first one: Dickens. So the children were dressed up as characters. There was limitless beer, and a spread laid out for all the children in the middle of Weller Way. The Pandemonium Band played. Max Steinberg of the Housing Corporation was there to snip the ribbon. 'Five years ago,' he began, 'my secretary said to me, there's a man called Billy Floyd wants to see you and he's very persistent...'

Before an afternoon and evening of eating and drinking Tom Phillips – who'd baked some of the food himself at home – was persuaded to unveil a plaque. (Later a search had to be launched for Tom, who was sleeping it off in somebody's flat.) Bill Halsall handed over an album of photographs of the co-op from start to finish.

There was a pause in the celebrations to remember Dickie Sharp. Then they went on, in the spirit in which the co-op had developed: together. There'd been a competition to decide what went on the plaque. Arthur Roberts' winning entry reads:

> Just a bit of everyone
> There's not much more to say
> We gave our time and leisure
> To show we're here to stay.

Others had proposed 'Housing for need not for greed' and, from Philip Hughes, 'From each according to his ability; to each according to his needs.' There was only one entry from a child: Karen Byrne, daughter of Ann and Kevin. The estate the co-op built is intended to last longer than Karen's lifetime. As one of the older ones, Kate Kelly, says: 'The young ones 'll be running this co-op in future years. They should be listened to: what they think, what they'd like to happen.' Here's Karen's poem about the co-op:

> We made our future by getting together and
> helping each other
>
> We knew we had it
> Right from the start
> The feeling came from
> deep down in our hearts
> We knew it was right
> When we got the site
> It lit up our lives
> We was so bright
> And now we remember
> the houses we had
> We write our memories
> down on a plaque

9

Where Dreams Are Ended

Most members of the co-op are very happy with life on the estate. A survey of their views in 1984 (based on the Department of the Environment's standard survey of tenant satisfaction) showed that Weller Streets members were far more satisfied with their estate than virtually all Council tenants. Or, as Joe McLennan says in his contented retirement: 'It's a little bit of heaven, this. I tell you, if Our Lord made anything better than this He kept it to Himself. This is the best time of my life.'

One former member of the co-op who now rents a house from a housing association expresses the ultimate achievement of the co-op this way: 'When you compare the house I'm living in now to Billy's house, or, say, a Council house, it's totally different. The people have designed the houses. Their ideas are in it; not some faceless wonder's.'

Bill Halsall reinforces the point. In developing the design, he felt, 'It came across they had a degree of idealism about their own community: trying to continue it in the same mould it had been at some time in the past, before it was corrupted.'

The ideas and idealism – the dream – lived in the houses. But the fight to achieve the dream had been different in nature from the eventual long-term task: the day-to-day job of managing the estate. There's a lot of routine work to do: collecting the rents, chasing up the arrears, keeping the books, organizing repairs. There's no fight with anyone out there any more. It's a question of getting on with one another: doing the gardens, maintaining the landscaping, sweeping out the courts, resolving disputes between people or factions.

Inevitably there was some sense of disappointment, of anti-climax among the old vanguard of the committee once they moved on to the estate. It's anticipated in Kevin Byrne's (rejected) suggestion for the plaque to commemorate the site opening. 'Build a future from yesterday' was the title, and the words:

> When dreams can appear so real?
> The answer lies where dreams are ended.

'They were occasionally rather sad,' said Max Steinberg of the Housing Corporation, 'because they couldn't always achieve what they set out to achieve.' Many of the core members of the committee, too, were simply exhausted by all the effort they'd put in, and were bewildered, when they began living on the estate, to find that they were still expected to shoulder the majority of the work burden. 'It still needs more commitment from a lot of people,' says Peter Tyrrell, who tried to cast off the role of chairman but was persuaded, after illness, to return. Kevin Byrne puts it more strongly: 'When I see it now, I often wonder where we went wrong. We could have done better... Some of the people and the kids, they're not looking after it... All the people who are living in it: they're not living up to their fucking promises. Oh, it's only untidy, but...'

It's clear that many of the day-to-day problems of management are precisely because the co-op's ideas are written into the bricks-and-mortar, are expressed in the fact of living next to one another on the estate. Unresolved conflicts within these ideas are the stuff of theses: but for co-op members they're the everyday arguments that have to be resolved.

Thus, for instance, the co-op, in its development period, was clearly more a 'collective' than a broadly based democratic organization. Members put their trust in a leadership, an inner cabinet that they believed represented them. 'They fought them bureaucrats in town'...'I can't praise the men enough for getting it done the way that it is'...'They put a hell of a lot of work in. The night after night they fought for us'...Time and again these are the sorts of things less active members will say of the committee. Ex-members Billy Odger and Harry Dono were discussing the issue one night. Billy said, 'Myself, I think that the people stuck together over it.' But in Harry's view: 'You say, "people", but the committee made it work.'

Yet built into the design were the separate courtyards, with their individual landscaping, based on the idea that once the houses were finished everyone would join in the running of the estate. As the co-op had written to the Rent Officer, in explaining their intent:

> Self-management will mostly be organized around the activities of individual courts, with each group of people co-operating amongst themselves. The overseeing and overall control of management and maintenance will remain with our management committee.

But it wasn't enough merely to state this as policy. It wasn't even enough to secure promises from the general membership that they would follow it through. For how could committee or general members unlearn overnight the roles they'd developed over the previous six years? When the rules of tenancy co-op members had themselves developed concentrated on what was or wasn't allowed? Not emphasizing the responsibilities of co-op members (for instance, there's no rule saying members should be involved in the communal maintenance of the landscaping)?

Thus the tension remains, and seems likely to remain, between the committee and the wider membership. The committee tries to attract new members and wants them to speak up. Kate Kelly recalls an argument at a committee meeting over a fund-raising issue: 'I had bloody murder with them. And Philip was made up. He said, "Why don't you come every Monday and get the women talking?"'

Yet when new members join the committee they find it difficult to break in, as Kitty reports: 'Now the men on the committee have stressed we need new faces. I think the women have been a little bit embarrassed. So they've come on to the committee. These new members don't say nothing. One girl has said things, but has said to me, she gets shouted down.'

Committee members sometimes complain about the lack of involvement of other members. Yet individual initiatives can be squashed if they don't meet the committee's approval. Philip Roberts tried to get a Gardening Club started. 'So I went round, fifty-one or fifty-two wanted to be on the Gardening Club. When I put the proposal to the management committee, I couldn't do it. It had to be under the control of the management committee. They said, "You can't be autonomous." So it sort of put me off.'

This tension was built into the design, into the organization of the co-op. A related problem has been that of maintaining the landscaping. History catches up with you: the landscaping had been organized when experienced co-op members were busy with other things, and the landscape architect had never seemed to have much time, and consultation with people in some courts had been hurried. The result: some of the courts had difficulty maintaining their landscaping. Kitty says, 'The problem is, a lot of us don't know a weed or a plant...See, none of us have had gardens. What they've got in their own gardens, they know what's there. But in the court they don't know what's in it.'

Some of the problems, too, resulted from misplaced optimism about how people's attitudes might change once they were living on the estate. As Peter Tyrrell reported to the

Annual General Meeting after a year of management, about damage done to the communal landscaping: 'The sad thing about this problem is that most of the damage has been done by our own children and their friends that they bring on to the Estate.'

'We missed that,' says Phil Roberts. 'We thought we'd control the kids. These kids, they live in the urban jungle like we were.' The seemingly minor savings when the landscaping was being done – no low fencing or trip rail around the court landscaping; no fees allowed to pay a landscape architect – came home to roost once the co-op were in management. Efforts to control the children couldn't wholly succeed. Kitty says, 'There's kids on the site wrecking the plants and people not coming out of their houses to tell them...I don't shout at them. I say, "Hey, lad, don't do that, you're spoiling it."'

But some pensioners are understandably nervous about talking to the older children. As one of them says, 'It's a shame the kids knock 'em down. You don't like to say anything 'cause they say, oh those old moaners...'

Some of these problems and arguments were, however, the inevitable, and not necessarily undesirable, effect of being a group of people managing their own housing together. As Kate Kelly puts it, 'Now we're actually on it we're starting the teething problems over again. Let's face it, if we all agreed, it wouldn't be a co-op.'

And in some ways the focus of the co-op's activity did shift in the transition from development to management; from the 'military' administration to the civil one. When Joe Corbett took a job working with co-ops for a housing association, Irene Stead became the co-op's part-time worker, dealing with day-to-day administration. Gradually the long-standing fund-raising committee, chaired by Kate, became less of a background way of involving less active members of the co-op; more, part of the fabric of the co-op itself, an expression of neighbourliness and solidarity.

And – more by accident than design – a group of women members gradually took over the oversight of the co-op's finances. Ever since Adrian Moran of CDS had first told them how they were going to borrow a million pounds, co-op members had felt nervous about the unreal-seeming sums of money they dealt in. Dickie Sharp, as treasurer, had relieved everyone else of the burden of this. He kept the books; the others signed the cheques. 'It's terrible,' says Philip Hughes, 'I haven't got two ha'pennies to rub together and I sign all this money away. The biggest one I had was £97,000.'

Dickie's death left a void which Kitty, then Irene, as treasurer, struggled to fill. But meanwhile a group of women had been drawn together in the summer of 1981 to work as a 'finance group' for the proposed secondary co-op. When the secondary died, they stayed together as a rent committee. Someone from the co-op's accountants taught them how to record the weekly rent payments; then, a couple of years later, how to do the book-keeping that the accountants had previously done for the co-op. Gradually, despite continuing awkwardness and misunderstandings between the finance committee and the management committee, they took over the figure-work.

It's important to remember that, in the midst of the problems, the disagreements and the hard work involved in running the co-op, for most members the realization of the dream was a marvellous achievement. As Sammy Roberts puts it: 'To come here – we're millionaires. We didn't realize we were coming to Utopia. Just wait till my mates on the docks see this. We're all toffs.'

Of course not everything's sweetness and light. There's been the trauma of threatening to take a member to court for their rent arrears; there've been the niggling problems of defects left over from the building contract. Nevertheless the idealism about their own community that Bill Halsall speaks of, the neighbourliness the co-op sought to achieve through their design and their way of organizing themselves have, substantially, been achieved. Ada Hewitt said: 'It's like one big family, that's the beauty of it. Everybody knows one another.'

Ada and her sister Lily Durrant lived in neighbouring flats in Birch Court: two people who got more involved in the co-op once it was built. Lily says, 'The young ones are very good. They always come in and say, what shopping d'you need? Especially Tina: we call her Mrs Seeyafter, 'cause she always says, see y'after. And we love the kiddies coming in.' One morning they had to use the alarm at 4 a.m. when Ada was taken ill. It sounded in the court and Peter Tyrrell came across. After that he popped in every Sunday to see they were okay.

The elderly being mixed in with the rest, instead of being segregated into a sheltered block of housing, has meant that, as Kitty puts it, 'Our pensioners don't class themselves as pensioners. That's why they're on the fund-raising with the young.' Edie McLennan recalled how at one point nobody tried to collect from the elderly for children's parties and days out. 'For a couple of weeks they didn't come, and they said, "Oh, we didn't think it was fair, asking the pensioners." And we said, "We have our pleasures in other ways, and we're glad."'

The way the elderly and the rest get on with one another, and the general feeling of neighbourliness, are repeatedly contrasted by people with what happens elsewhere. Those who've left feel the absence of it. 'You miss the neighbours, that's all,' says Ada Odger. 'You miss the faces.' Harry Dono recalls how 'There was always something going on. Like Kitty Kelly 'd always get a bus together. I miss that part of it.'

Rozzie Lybert compares what's happened to her, in the coop, with other people she knew: 'My next-door neighbour, she's gone to [a housing association house in] Gwendoline Street: she loves it. Somebody else, they've gone out to [a Council house in] Old Swan: they're going to buy it when the three years are up. And yet, I've asked those same people, do they miss their old houses. "Yes I do, I miss Pecksniff Street – the atmosphere

– you don't go to the front door and talk to people." Whereas like here, in the summer, they're all in one another's gardens.'

Whatever the problems with the communal landscaping, the individual gardens have been a great success. For people who'd only ever had a backyard all their lives, it was both exciting and a bit nerve-racking to have a garden. Joe McLennan, for instance, had never thought he'd fancy one. 'But once we got down here it was like a little magnet. We grew potatoes, tomatoes, cabbages. I never thought I'd have green fingers but I have, more than I ever thought.'

Tom Phillips, the ex-clerk of works, gave Joe and Edie a lot of help with their garden. At first, he says 'they expected to see something growing the next day. They didn't have the patience... They were pulling them out of the ground 'cause they said they were no good. They didn't give them a chance to grow bigger.' As with the landscaping, people expected instant results, instant greenery; they only slowly got used to the time and patience required to make things grow.

And it has, perhaps, been the same with the co-op itself. The idea behind it was to keep the community together in decent housing. And yet, as Sammy Roberts says of the community, 'To tell the truth it was only strong when we formed this co-op.' He thinks that living there has made more people involved. 'There's people doing more now, now they've got their own place, than they were doing before.' They've made the dream real by their own collective efforts. Living there, they're still building on the vision.

Meanwhile, in the seven years it took for the Weller Streets to put their ideas into their housing, the idea of 'a housing co-operative' was continuing to develop a life of its own – which meant, on Merseyside, a sometimes farcical and bizarre one. Housing co-operatives became an industry employing professionals; a hot political issue; an academic subject.

The separation of the idea from the bricks and mortar wasn't something confined to professionals and politicians. As Peter Tyrrell expresses his motivation: 'It was mainly the fight, mainly the idea: Let's take *them* on, let's see who *they* are – 'cause your life had been fucking dominated by people you never knew. So I thought, that's for me. Let's have a go at *them*.'

Some members carried this further. Steve Cossack – though he became a resident member – says he was never that interested in a house, more in the idea. Stephen Rice left the co-op, with some bitterness, before the estate was completed. 'Since then,' he says, 'I've seen much better co-operatives: far more harmony, better organized... They'll be a far better example of co-operatives than the Weller Streets: better organization, more cohesion, more flexibility, and also a greater proportion of the people in the co-operative being involved in the business of it.'

The Weller Streets was never, from its inception, going to be the broadly based kind of group Stephen had in mind. There was always a gulf between the leading members and the rest – a gulf Stephen more than most tried to bridge – a gulf which most general members were not unhappy with. As Hilda Mills puts it: 'It's about the only [group] I've heard of where neighbours have been like that; put so much into it to get it off the ground... At the meetings they argued with one another. And they're the ones that were running it. You've got to put your point of view.' *You* put your point of view: *they* were running it.

The new-build co-ops that spawned from the Weller Streets' example in Liverpool – working with CDS and other housing associations – have only rarely followed this model, of an inner core of leaders, responsible in a collective way to the less active wider membership. But certainly it was the Weller Streets' initial example that helped to fire people's enthusiasm, and to show that the 'crazy idea' could become a reality. Paul Lusk of CDS himself found his initial enthusiasm for co-ops in the

Weller Streets. Five years on, he said, 'What's happening now, in Liverpool, is that a new form of public sector housing is being developed. And it's not just co-ops, it's new-build co-ops. Only through new building do you have the opportunity to shape an environment. And it's going to be the – a major, possibly dominant – form of public housing in the twentieth century. And the Weller Streets will have been the model.'

The Weller Streets are a reluctant 'model' for anyone. This is one source of the lingering dissatisfaction leading members have felt: that their experience has been used by others to advance causes they don't believe in. Their own effort to form a 'secondary' co-op, where co-operatives would themselves pool their experience and resources, independent of professionals, failed. They've remained the only new-build group in Liverpool to go wholly their own way, without a housing association as their agent. They opposed CDS's idea of forming co-ops among local authority tenants, seeing it as, in Peter Tyrrell's words, 'assisting the Corpie to manage their fucking shite'. They knew CDS had learnt along with co-op members and resented professional control by stealth. Here, for example, is an extract from the 1981 CDS paper on management co-ops over which the two groups finally fell out:

> While self-management through voluntary effort obviously plays a part in all co-ops, experience suggests that only the smallest co-ops (say fifty units or less) will find it practical to do all the work for themselves. Above a certain size, it is more efficient to use professional services for most tasks. For example, rent collection can easily be handled by self-help by ten households, but a hundred families will probably find it more practical to pay someone to carry out the work.

CDS were referring to other, reported 'experience' in talking about what was more 'practical' and 'efficient'. The Weller Streets' subsequent experience was, indeed, to refute the argument: the women on the Finance Committee balance up the co-op's sixty-one rents every week, and could efficiently handle double that (though it'd cut down the time they have for a glass of lager afterwards).

But the Weller Streets never found a way of working with their fellow co-ops to share their knowledge and experience. They send representatives along to the local federation, but have often been regarded there as oddballs, the socialists, the sometimes rather arrogant pioneers. Only after several years have they mellowed enough to deal with CDS again – helping them with training courses.

Chiefly it's the professionals who learn from one co-op, to pass on their experience to another. CDS have worked with many co-ops since the Weller Streets. 'They've been a demonstration, a way forward, the first of their generation,' says Catherine Meredith. But she adds: 'You can't take the Weller Streets as a model, because of the time demands.' The professionals' inexperience, the fact that they were learning along with the Weller Streets, helped to make it work. But when the 'model' is applied to other groups in other circumstances, that naivety can't be carried along with it. Enthusiasm becomes more muted. You have to be 'realistic' about the demands on your time. There are other meetings to get to.

As Max Steinberg of the Housing Corporation puts it: 'In essence they thought, and I think still believe, that they beat the system in some way. I think in fact the system proved it could work for groups like them.' In the course of the notion of 'a housing co-operative' gaining wider currency, the idea itself gets flattened out, reduced to something like a formula. And in the process – perhaps the inevitable process, if co-ops are to be more than unique experiments – the broader involvement of co-op members that Stephen Rice espoused leads in many cases to co-ops choosing between options decided by the professionals, whereas the leading members of the Weller Streets actually created the options themselves.

In the context of this experience the Weller Streets, especially after the failure of the secondary co-op, turned inwards, away from the propagation of the idea of co-ops, to their own self-management: back, indeed, to what first motivated them, the desire to better their own housing conditions. One sign of this greater introspection has been the changing proposals for the site of the photographic works neighbouring the estate (burnt down in mysterious circumstances while the estate was being built). Originally the co-op had wanted a community centre on the site, a centre for the whole area. But eventually, faced by rejection of their plea for funds for this from the Inner City Partnership, they settled on a proposal for another courtyard.

In trying to get finance for this proposal they faced, in a series of ironic twists, the way the idea of a housing co-operative had taken on a life of its own, and the fact that history catches up with you. For first, over several years, they sought funds from the Housing Corporation, who'd financed and therefore held on mortgage the rest of the estate. It seemed the logical thing to do.

The Housing Corporation consistently turned them down. Naturally they were given sound administrative reasons for this: the pressure of other demands on limited funds, the importance of meeting other, more pressing, housing needs. But it's surely no coincidence that Billy Floyd had manhandled and threatened the local boss of the Housing Corporation, when the co-op had performed their commando raid of the Atlantic Tower to talk to the Housing Corporation's Chairman. Short-term gains sometimes lead to long-term defeats.

Instead, logic would have dictated that the Weller Streets should seek funding from the local Council. But by now the Labour party were in charge, after years of Liberal–Conservative control. Leading members of the Weller Streets had never had much time for the Liberals' espousal of housing co-ops, which had run alongside a programme of no new Council house-building. As Kitty Heague put it: 'The Liberals don't seem to realize a co-op's not the answer to Liverpool's housing problems.' Or Steve Cossack: 'The Liberals are off-loading their responsibility. One thing we've never said in this co-op is, Co-ops are the only answer. It was the answer for us. It's just, effectively, public housing.'

But, once Labour came into power locally in 1983 – just as the Thatcher government was being voted into a second term of office nationally – there was to be none of the subtlety in developing a policy towards co-ops that Weller Streets members might have wanted. For the Liverpool Labour Party co-ops were a Liberal-sponsored diversion from the real issues. Co-ops were out. The Weller Streets got no funding from the Council, even though, as Paul Lusk observed of the leading committee members: 'They saw themselves as socialists in a much more specific way than other groups do. Their image of their estate was rented housing. They were very clear they didn't want to look like a Barratt's estate. And the impulse towards egalitarianism is very much a part of that.'

One member, Tina Caveney, interviewed before the estate was completed, said, 'We all know what we're going there for, and there'll be no bitchiness because we all realize that we're a working-class group and we all have the same as each other.' But the Liverpool Labour Party felt unable to recognize co-ops as legitimate 'working-class groups'. As Tony Byrne (no relation), Chairman of the Council's Finance Committee and the man behind its housing policy, said in a newspaper interview:

> I am a Socialist. I believe in public ownership, control and accountability for housing through the elected council. It is the local authority who must satisfy the needs of the working class. Working-class organization in this city lies in the Labour Party and the unions, and not in housing associations.

So Labour have, in Liverpool, mounted a major five-year

programme of investment in Council housing without involving co-ops, and with a bare minimum of consultation with tenants. Councillor Byrne thinks co-ops represent the old 'consensus politics that have failed'. Yet the Weller Streets – whose leading members are of a similar age, and share the same Liverpool working-class background and broad attitudes as many Labour councillors – discovered for themselves that a co-op was the precise opposite: an attack on the old consensus that regarded housing as a simple choice between owner-occupation for the better-off and municipal housing for the rest. Distrust of the local authority, whatever political party controlled it, was a driving force in their development. A new kind of 'working-class organization', through the co-op, was for them the only way they could get what they wanted.

The ironies of this outcome are profound. The Weller Streets and other co-ops find their potential financial support from the Conservative government. It's the Conservative Secretary of State who in the interests of 'diversity' and 'self-help' wants to keep supporting co-ops in Liverpool. It's HRH The Prince of Wales who, with a newly discovered enthusiasm for 'community architecture', has visited the Weller Streets – another day for great celebration – and has then gone away to make speeches about the potential co-ops might realize:*

It seemed to me that if only we could enable more people, especially in the inner city areas, to develop the kind of self-confidence I had seen with my own eyes in the sort of places of which most authorities and agencies tend to despair, that self-confidence, from the discovery of previously hidden talents and abilities, could spill over into other regenerative enterprises...

Further afield there's been support from the Labour Party.

*He was there to unveil a plaque commemorating the Housing Centre Trust's Golden Jubilee Award, won for 'outstanding housing achievement in Britain 1980–1984'.

Jeff Rooker, the Shadow Housing spokesman, visited the estate. The speech he's been touring the country with, laying out Labour's future national housing policy, is substantially different from the local view:

> Labour sees housing co-ops as flagships for change towards tenant participation and freedom in rented housing. We shall give firm government support to co-ops where tenants collectively own the accommodation but no individual holds a stake. We shall seek for all tenants real control over their homes and we do not mean the colour of paint on the front door. We mean design, repair priorities, allocation policies, etc.

After all the twists and turns that their 'dream' has been subjected to, it's small wonder that the Weller Streets finally agree about their own supposed uniqueness. 'The Weller Streets 'll always be a one-off,' says Kevin Byrne. Professionals talk about the co-op's 'colourful characters'; they and co-op members alike debate the 'special chemistry' which made the Weller Streets work.

Certainly the particular circumstances which made the co-op work are unrepeatable. Being pioneers made it both more difficult, and more exciting, than for others who follow. The professionals were learning along with the co-op. The members acted as foils to one another: Philip Hughes keeping the chairman in check; Kitty and Irene telling the men what they didn't understand about women; the quieter members of the post-war generation – Arthur Roberts, Billy Odger, Harry Dono – keeping the hotheads in check; the older generation providing a steadying hand.

And there were always jokes to ease the seriousness, from Kate Kelly to Billy Floyd, from Kitty Heague to Philip Hughes: a natural Liverpool style that can't be high-minded without taking the piss as well. Kevin Byrne is famous for leading the design, but also for the night he took the wind out of the sails of a visiting sociology student who talked about 'ordinary people'. There were some women's clothes lying around, ready for a rummage sale. He tried on a dress and, pulling on the Lurex gloves to match, said to the student, 'What about me: d'you think I'm ordinary?'

The point is, they achieved something quite extraordinary. Through considerable intelligence and creativity the Weller Streets forged a radically new way of developing, designing and owning housing. Some of them are exhausted or permanently changed by all the effort they put in. Some of them can hardly believe just how much ability they discovered in themselves. They boast of the aggression that got them what they wanted – when it was the cunning and realism behind the aggression that won victories for them.

And now the ironies multiply. While the professionals prosper – Bill Halsall and Gordon Tait are partners in their firms; Catherine Meredith was awarded an MBE – times have got harder. Many co-op members, like Philip Hughes and Kevin Byrne, are more or less permanently unemployed now. And their 'vision' seems to have got distorted or lost along the way. The local Labour Party outlaws co-ops; some of their allies are to be found in the strangest places.

It's the commitment and energy, the talent and the 'chemistry' that make people say the Weller Streets are unique. Certainly nobody else could do it quite their way. But what sounds like a compliment can also be a way of dismissing the co-op. Their supposedly 'unique' achievement questions the role of middle-of-the-road professional, left-wing activist and right-wing politician alike. For lightning didn't strike a small corner of Liverpool one starry night and spark genius in a dozen homes. Talent like theirs is buried in Council blocks, in offices and on the shop floor, in the under-achievers at school and the under-employed in the dole queue. The co-op happens to have been a rare opportunity for a group of working-class people to demonstrate what society is burying.

Postscript: *Getting to the Bones of It*:
Being Reported On

Every account of what the Weller Streets have achieved will leave someone dissatisfied. Obviously this book will be no exception. Memories differ; the author's bias intrudes; there's always a gulf between re-imagining what happened and how it felt to be there.

From the beginning the originality of the Weller Streets attracted a good deal of public attention. From the first article about the co-op (in the then community newspaper *Liverpool 8 Express*, by one Joe Corbett, in November 1977), there's been a steady stream of media publicity and academic scrutiny.

In Billy Floyd's view, despite all this attention, 'Nobody's ever got to the bones of it. They've just taken little pieces which is useful to the medium. Like, the papers wanted to take pictures of the kids dressed as chimney-sweeps. Nobody wanted to know about the fucking boring balls-aching meetings in freezing rooms. Nobody wanted to know how stupid we felt when Meredith or Moran were saying, "Don't you understand? – Okay, we'll explain it to you again." That's what people should be getting told. Not, if you all stick together there's an easy simple formula for how you do it.'

Publicity is a double-edged sword. With experience the co-op became as sophisticated in public relations as they were in design. Publicity was used to help exert political pressure, and in 'putting on a front' to both public bodies and to the less involved general membership: demonstrating that the Weller

Streets were a viable, publicly accepted institution. So kids dressed as chimney-sweeps helped to get media attention, but also led to superficial coverage. Putting over a confident, positive image meant that only the most searching questioner would report 'how stupid we felt'.

Part of the frustration Billy Floyd talks about stems, too, from the false situations press and TV conjure up. Philip Roberts recalls the mechanics of making a Granada film (set up in 1980 to get some publicity when it looked like everything might fall apart for lack of a builder): 'I was talking to him about fifteen or twenty minutes. When it came on the telly there was no sound, just me pointing. Three or four seconds on the box, like.'

Later there was part of a 'community' BBC TV programme devoted to the Weller Streets. The producer wanted to set up a shot of Kevin and Billy going to a meeting. But there was a problem with the light, so he asked them to walk in a different direction. 'That's not the way I go to the meeting,' said Kevin, and refused to do it. Billy adds, of the producer: 'He seemed a nice guy. Talking to him it seemed as if he had his finger on it. He was saying, "What you think is good television isn't good television." We were thinking, he's got enough on film to make it really representative. But it wasn't.'

Press and television, in the nature of things, used the Weller Streets to make 'good television' or 'good copy'. It's perhaps not surprising, then, that the press coverage leading members of the co-op regarded as good tended to be 'feature articles', where the journalists concerned could take time to listen and learn, and to check back their text with the co-op. One such was a *Guardian* article by Robert Waterhouse in 1978. 'He spent a couple of days down here really listening,' says Billy Floyd. Another was an article by Nick Wates, four years later, in the *Architect's Journal*. Again the reporter took time to spend with the co-op on the story. Again he sent a draft to the co-op. 'The things we objected to were omitted,' says Peter Tyrrell.

Peter was centrally involved as spokesman for the co-op, first as press officer, later as chairman. He says of the majority of reporters: 'They'd come down, they'd talk to them. When you read the article you just couldn't believe the crap they fucking wrote: nothing in it that was what you'd talked to them about. They'd come down and say, "How's the system fucking assisted you?" And the system hadn't given us anything. We had to wring everything out of them.'

Peter here puts his finger on the most fundamental objection to the way the co-op has been reported on: that journalists and academics came to the co-op with pre-conceived ideas, and then used selective quotes in order to peddle these ideas instead of listening to the range of ideas co-op members wanted to express. Peter particularly recalls a reporter for a local paper: 'I had a meeting with him and he just didn't want to know the fucking struggles we had to do it. He just wanted a pretty story. He got a right cob on.'

Academic reporting on the co-op has suffered from the same problems. Much of it has been done by students who are future professionals. They've mostly been listened to politely, been given facilities to interview, and then never been seen again; though if they came over as condescending, some of the committee resorted to deliberately disconcerting them (as in Kevin's antics with the Lurex gloves quoted on p. 214).

One limitation of academic reporting is that the results are intended for an alien, academic audience. Thus, for example, Rob Macdonald worked closely with the co-op in its early stages, taking comprehensive minutes, and, in Billy Floyd's words, 'became part of the co-op, like an honorary member'. Yet when he came to write about his research in a paper the work had to be translated into a language which hardly any ordinary human being could understand. 'The paper', says part of his introduction to it, 'concentrates upon the theoretical implications of taking a phenomenological stance in Man-environment studies, the methodology of participant observation, and the creation of original data about the inside of the English working-class home...'

Tony Gibson of Nottingham University took a different approach. He too began by offering something to the co-op: game-playing to stimulate self-education. One of his card games, which much of the general membership enjoyed, became the basis for the formulation of the co-op's tenancy agreement. He visited the co-op a lot, tape-recording interviews and events, building up from these recordings a 'fact pack' of what the co-op had done, and quotations from committee members, to be offered to other community groups.

But even after he'd spent hundreds of hours visiting the co-op, many leading members felt dissatisfied with what he'd done. Some felt he wasn't really on their wave-length. As Philip Hughes puts it: 'He doesn't talk our language. He didn't understand what we were talking about.' Kevin Byrne: 'He's riding on the back of what we're doing. He's on a nice comfortable living.'

Ironically this was the impression Tony Gibson left behind, rather than the truth of the matter. 'I don't make any living out of Weller Streets,' he says (in a letter to the Publishing Company responding to these criticisms). 'I used part of what I earned elsewhere to subsidize material about Weller Streets for the benefit of other groups.' Clearly he was and is an enthusiast for the co-op as an example of 'people power'. Perhaps it was over-enthusiasm, and a tendency to simplify when writing about the Weller Streets for a wider audience, that provoked a comment like Peter Tyrrell's: 'He wouldn't go away. His first exercise was helpful to us: the card game. But he just kept coming and coming. People told him to piss off in the end. There's still people here deal with him, and that's all right. I just don't want to know.'

Some of the 'people here' who still deal with him include a group of women, among them Kitty and Irene, who participated in a feature insert for 'Woman's Hour' that Tony Gibson put together. He checked back the proposed programme with them, and they were all happy with it. They didn't share the view Billy Floyd expresses: 'Gibson's problem all along was he already had what he wanted in his head; then unravelled it back, then sort of claimed the people were doing that. I think most of his stuff's like that.'

This opinion of his work is akin to the feeling co-op members had about journalistic reporting, and indeed about how the example of the Weller Streets had been used to further the growth of co-ops in Liverpool. Outsiders had used the Weller Streets' experience as propaganda for their own points of view. In generalizing about that experience they'd planed away the rough edges that, to leading co-op members, were what made the experience uniquely their own.

Rob Macdonald said of his reporting on the co-op: 'I consciously set out not to write about what they were doing. I thought it important that at some time they did it themselves.' Nobody in the co-op ended up actually writing the story themselves. Instead they employed me to do it.

I'd worked for the Housing Corporation and for CDS. By August 1982 I was a freelance writer when, through a chance meeting with Bill Halsall, Billy Floyd made contact with me. The outcome was that a private company was set up, the Weller Streets Publishing Company. The only people who can hold shares in the company are residents of the co-op: the vast majority of residents are shareholders. The company twisted the arms of a few of the 'professionals' involved to finance paying me to write the co-op's story. Copyright of the book rests with the Publishing Company, not me.

Clearly this accountability to co-op members can't get over all the problems the Weller Streets had recognized in the way they'd been reported on before. Interviews and quotations are selective. I sought out leading members and ex-members of the co-op, rather than trying to interview every co-op member. I interviewed 'professionals' but not politicians. While drafts of the book were circulated to members of the co-op interested or involved, the right was reserved to me to present the balance of views I chose. While Billy Floyd had talked at the outset of a 'warts and all' story, the descriptions of a small number of events have been disguised out of consideration for the people involved.

Peter Tyrrell says that reporters who've come to the co-op 'won't ever get it right. I think there's been a fair few good attempts at getting it right. The only fucking reason for doing this [book] is that people have misused, have got it wrong before. They're doing it for what they get out of it themselves. The other crowd, who say they're going to do wonders for you: they just go away.'

Perhaps in the end this book is just another of the 'fair few good attempts'. Bill Halsall only made paper houses; the members of the Weller Streets have to live in them. This is only a paper story; it was and is a part of their lives. But at least the houses belong to them now; and so, too, does the extraordinary story of how that was achieved.

Appendix:

A Timetable of Events

1977

June — Working party meets to discuss the co-op idea.

August — First meeting of the Weller Streets Housing Co-op.

November — Council offers Hesketh Street site.

December — Co-op registered as a housing association.

1978

January — Co-op informally offered Miles/Byles site.

April — Council formally offers Miles/Byles site to co-op.

April — Architects appointed.

May — Revised Sub-committees, including Inside and Outside design committees, set up.

September — Co-op signs development agreement with CDS Liverpool.

1979

January — Co-op rejects alternative design.

February — Meeting with the city engineers over 'adoption' of roads.

April — THIS LAND NOW BELONGS TO THE PEOPLE

June — Detailed proposals sent to the Housing Corporation.

July — Joe Corbett, full-time worker, appointed.

September   'Tripartite' meeting with Housing Corporation
             and Department of the Environment.
November   Disagreements with architect over programme.

1980
February   'Burning the Boats' meeting where co-op mem-
             bers choose co-op or local authority rehousing.
February   Housing Corporation approves going out to tender.
April   Tenders invited for building contract.
August   Building contract signed. Work starts on site.
             Tom Phillips, clerk of works, appointed.
November   Raid on Atlantic Tower to meet chairman of
             Housing Corporation.

1981
April   Co-op breaks off its agreement with CDS.
August   Collapse of 'secondary' co-op.
October   First handovers of completed dwellings.

1982
October   Last tenants move in.